Praise for *Called*

"Ryan perfectly captures the roller coaster of mixed emotions you really experience when you dare to answer one of God's big questions for your life, 'What if?' There's an adventure hidden in this book and one inside you too. Read Ryan's words to find both."

— **Jon Acuff**, *New York Times* bestselling author of *Start: Punch Fear in the Face, Escape Average & Do Work that Matters*

"With a poignant and unflinching voice, Ryan Pemberton brings a fresh perspective to the winding and often complex journey of faith. His writing brings to mind the work of Donald Miller, mixed with the vulnerability of my favorite stories from NPR's "This American Life." Pemberton is a thinking Christian who does not shy away from thought provoking questions about faith. He is a writer to watch and I eagerly await his next work. Quietly powerful and inspiring, *Called: My Journey To C. S. Lewis's House and Back Again* is a memoir that is not to be missed."

— **Michael Morris**, author of *Man in the Blue Moon, Slow Way Home,* and *A Place Called Wiregrass*

"In this finely written memoir, Ryan Pemberton takes us into the halls and streets and stories of magical, historic Oxford, and into the life and home of its renowned thinker-poet C. S. Lewis. As we follow Ryan on his quest to find what it means to be called, with all the excitement and doubt and second-guessing that entails, *we* are the ones who make the discovery that in the end, calling isn't so much about a grand task or an exciting journey, but about listening, trust, and deep surrender."

— **Sheridan Voysey**, writer, speaker, broadcaster, and author of *Resurrection Year: Turning Broken Dreams into New Beginnings.* www.sheridanvoysey.com

"Like David the young Psalmist, Ryan knows how to write and has something to say. Intelligent, personal, and refreshingly honest, Ryan's warm heart, active mind, and hungry soul shine through on every page, illuminating what is often a dimly lit path towards knowing and doing God's will. A worthy read."

—**Dick Staub**, author, broadcaster, founder *The Kindlings Muse,* and a Country Parson on Orcas Island

"I cannot think of a memoir I have related to more than Ryan Pemberton's *Called.* It's a book I could not put down, not only because I have deep fondness for Lewis and Oxford but also because I sympathize with the unpredictable rhythms of life and calling that Ryan so eloquently captures. Calling unfurls itself more often as a twisty roller coaster than a smooth, open road. With honesty, passion and Narnia-like wonder, Ryan shows us in *Called* how beautifully thrilling the ride can be."

—**Brett McCracken**, author of *Gray Matters* (Baker Books, 2013) and *Hipster Christianity* (Baker Books, 2010)

"Oxford. C. S. Lewis. Living at the Kilns. An aspiring writer. A young marriage. A life of faith. These are the ingredients of what proved to be a most enjoyable memoir. Ryan Pemberton takes you right into Oxford's stately halls, he opens up doors to occasional C. S. Lewis tidbits that even many seasoned scholars haven't seen, and he weaves a tale of faith, love, hope and life to create a delightful and entertaining journey."

—**Gary Thomas**, author of *Sacred Marriage* and *A Lifelong Love*

"*Called* is beautiful and heart wrenching. It's a breath of fresh air for the generations raised to equate divine calling with radical adventure. Pemberton offers a rare invitation to slow down, recognize our humanity, and rely on God's faithfulness. He could be the *genuine* radical of the twentysomethings. Readers will appreciate his honesty as he tells the story of living in the home of his hero, C. S. Lewis where he learned a profound lesson—that our calling is to trust God's persistent love, and that it is through the painful stutter-steps of life, we hear Jesus say, 'Follow me.'"

—**Laura Anderson Kurk**, MA, author of *Glass Girl* and *Perfect Glass*

"Calling is complex and few have unraveled it as well as Pemberton. *Called* is an impassioned testimony that shows what it means to follow Jesus—it's inspiring, witty, honest, and brave. Pemberton will help you change your life for the better."

—**John D. Barry**, CEO of Jesus' Economy, editor of Faithlife Study Bible, and author

"I must confess that when Ryan first told me about his experience in the land of Lewis, I was more than a bit jealous. But as I started reading *Called*, that jealously quickly began to disappear. Ryan's writing is so vivid and so immersive that I felt like I was right there with him in England, enjoying magical dinners at the Kilns and roaming through the hallowed halls of Oxford University.

For anyone who has ever dreamed of walking in the footsteps of C. S. Lewis, but has been unable to make the voyage across the pond, this book is an absolute must read."

—**Zack Hunt**, blogger at *The American Jesus*

Called

Called

My Journey

— to —

C. S. LEWIS'S HOUSE

— and —

Back Again

Ryan J. Pemberton

LEAFWOOD
PUBLISHERS
an imprint of Abilene Christian University Press

CALLED
My Journey to C. S. Lewis's House and Back Again

LEAFWOOD
PUBLISHERS
an imprint of Abilene Christian University Press

Copyright © 2015 by Ryan J. Pemberton

ISBN 978-0-89112-384-2

Printed in the United States of America

LIBRARY OF CONGRESS CATALOGING-IN-PUBLICATION DATA
Pemberton, Ryan J., 1984-
  Called : my journey to C. S. Lewis's house and back again / Ryan J. Pemberton.
    pages cm
  Includes bibliographical references and index.
  ISBN 978-0-89112-384-2 (alk. paper)
  1. Vocation--Christianity. 2. Pemberton, Ryan J., 1984- 3. Lewis, C. S. (Clive Staples),
1898-1963. I. Title.
  BV4740.P46 2015
  248.4--dc23
                                                                    2014045221

Cover design by ThinkPen Design, Inc.
Interior text design by Sandy Armstrong, Strong Design

Leafwood Publishers is an imprint of Abilene Christian University Press
ACU Box 29138
Abilene, Texas 79699
1-877-816-4455 toll free
www.leafwoodpublishers.com

15 16 17 18 19 20 / 7 6 5 4 3 2 1

Contents

For Jen—
Without you
these words
would not be.

"[Vocation] comes from the Latin word *vocare*, to call, and means the work a man is called to by God.

There are all different kinds of voices calling you to all different kinds of work, and the problem is to find out which is the voice of God rather than of Society, say, or the Superego, or Self-Interest.

By and large a good rule for finding out is this. The kind of work God usually calls you to is the kind of work (*a*) that you need most to do and (*b*) that the world most needs to have done. . . . The place God calls you to is the place where your deep gladness and the world's deep hunger meet."

—Frederick Buechner, *Wishful Thinking: A Theological ABC*

Introduction

ob Dylan once said a poem is a naked person. I'm not much of a poet, but I hope you'll excuse me if I go ahead and take off all these layers.

This is a story of dreams coming true. It is a story of love and loss and adventure. It is a story of new life. But in the end, this is a story of how I failed, and what I learned about what it means to be called by the living God.

The cramped room smelled musty, like an ignored closet shut up for far too long. The blinds on the windows were pulled taut, refusing to let in much of any light. Other people were sprinkled around the room, all quietly waiting their turn to be seen.

It had been several years since my wife and I liquidated our retirement accounts in the worst economy since the Great Depression and left our jobs and the only home we had ever known to set out in pursuit of what we believed to be God's call on my life. This call had led us on a journey to England, to the

school of my dreams. It had meant having the kind of experiences I would not have believed possible had someone shared
them with me before we left.

But now I found myself back in the States, resting my head
against the brick wall in the back row of a social services waiting
room, reflecting on how I had gotten there. Seated beside my
wife and our baby girl—who had yet to celebrate her first birthday—I felt as though this was the end of our journey. And yet,
in a very real way, I realized then that it was also the beginning.

It was in that quiet waiting room, where the eyes of people
silenced by humiliation bored holes into the carpet, that I
realized what our journey had meant. Even though the scene
amounted to nothing short of my worst nightmare, a peace surrounded me on that afternoon. It was the kind of peace that's
only properly described as surpassing all understanding. It's the
kind of peace that puts a smile on your face when you might otherwise feel like crying. The peace that makes you kiss your wife
on her forehead, the only other person in the world who knows
just as well as you do what this journey has cost. It is the inex-
plicable peace that makes you smile at your daughter, with her
apple-cheeked grin staring back at you, recognizing for the first
time that *this* is what it means to follow the living Son of God.

I had spent the entirety of my short life running from the
poverty of this room. But it was only here that I learned what it
means to be called. It means, in a way I would not have believed
before we set out on this journey, that even sitting in my worst
nightmare, I wouldn't have it any other way.

1

Origins

An Unexpected Journey

You would completely misunderstand all I'm about to tell you if you didn't first know that studying theology at Oxford represents the complete opposite of everything I ever wanted growing up. If someone had told me when I was in high school that I'd one day leave a great job and move to England to study theology, I would have said they were crazy. That is, after I asked what "theology" is.

You see, I grew up in the far, far northwest corner of the States, in a valley that's home to row after row of raspberry plants and corn fields and dairy farms. My hometown lies somewhere halfway between the Cascades mountain range and the Pacific Ocean, where dairy cows outnumber people ten to one, and the lone blinking stoplight is more of a luxury than a necessity. The oldest of three, I played the role of son, brother, and father from a young age, wishing things were easier, more like the homes of other kids I knew. I remember Top Ramen and asking my mom how long we'd have to use food stamps and her silent, angry face. I remember standing in the outfield with my mitt on my hand wishing my dad was there, behind the chain-link fence with the other dads. I longed for my real dad, not one of the men who would stay with us for a month or two, maybe longer, with their strange, unfamiliar smells and habits. Those men who would teach me some things, and then fade away like the memory of a dream.

It took me a long time to realize I spend most days trying to not be that little boy. I still cannot eat Top Ramen.

My mom's hair is the color of sunshine, hanging from her head in a heap of curls, with a golden smile to match. My mom loved people, and she showed me the importance of helping others. When she was in high school, she worked with kids whose brains and arms and legs didn't work right. That's where I got my name, Ryan, she'd tell me. From one of those kids. "He had a beautiful spirit," she'd later tell me. I met him when I was in college. He was stooped over, with tufts of grey hair on his head, light blue circles around his eyes, and drool hanging from his mouth. I had no idea what to say. And he didn't talk.

We moved a lot growing up. I had probably lived in a dozen different homes (if not more) by the time I was in middle school. Mostly in the same town, though not always. I was a freshman in high school when I stopped unpacking all my boxes, leaving a stack in my closet that I didn't bother with. My mom always seems happy in my memories. But she wasn't. Not all the time. Sometimes I think those of us who seem most happy are actually hurting the most. I remember finding bottles under the sink and late night drives, praying we'd make it home safely. I remember waking up in the middle of the night as a young boy and finding my mom at the neighbors' house, sitting on a chair in the kitchen wearing nothing but a blue, scratchy tarp, refusing to look at me. There were times when she'd have to go away, and my brother and I would stay with my grandfather for a while.

My father was trained as an electrical engineer in the Air Force. Later, he worked on lasers for big companies that made computers. He lived in Vermont, California, and Texas, and his work often took him overseas: England, Korea, Germany. I did not know why we weren't together, my mom, my dad, and me. I would see my dad once or twice a year, and he'd send packages in between. Once, I received a letter from my father, accompanied by a photo of him standing in front of Stonehenge, his shoulders hugging his ears against the wind. He'd send mixtapes, too—U2, The Police, and Genesis. I'd listen to the words, "I could walk to your house, walking on the moon," on the Walkman my dad had also sent while I waited for the school bus, and I'd picture my dad walking on the moon. When an older boy asked to listen, I told him I got it from my dad. He asked if my dad had made the music and I realized I didn't know. So I told him he did.

I remember seeing a commercial for green Moon Shoes as a young boy, with smiling kids bouncing high into the air and laughing. I remember thinking, *I've got to get my hands on a pair of those.* A while later, I finally saw those Moon Shoes in an oversized box in the toy store and I walked away disappointed. There's no way those things would get me to the moon, I realized.

When I visited my dad in Vermont—I was five the first time I flew cross-country on my own—he'd take me for a ride on his motorcycle. Cringing at the sound of thunder at night, he'd tell me that I didn't have to be afraid, that it couldn't get us inside. I would watch him struggle on the lake with his windsurfing board. "Not enough wind today," he'd tell me afterward. In

California, we would travel all day in the car, and then spend the following day at amusement parks. And when he flew to Washington to see me, we'd share a large plate of nachos from a pub, play pool, watch movies, and I'd always wonder why he had to talk to everyone. Especially the women. Once, when he picked me up from the airport—his car always smelled like we were the first ones to use it—he took me to the mall and told me I could pick out some clothes. I told the woman working there that I wanted the outfit the plastic, headless white body wore. A week later, I flew home. I remember standing outside, looking at our trailer of a home, still wearing my new shirt, missing my father, and wondering why things had to be this way.

Growing up, my grandfather stood in for my dad in many ways. He taught me which is a Phillips-head and which is a flat-head screwdriver. He taught me the Lord's Prayer, and he told me that if I see something that needs to be done, I should go ahead and do it without waiting to be asked. The smells of fresh-cut wood and Coppertone sunscreen float through my memories of summers spent working on projects around the house with my grandfather. Since he has been retired for as far back as I can remember, we'd often spend our time together working on projects, like fixing things at the children's museum, where there was a full-size wooden train, and an oversized mouth with grotesque teeth and a punching bag for an uvula that you could crawl into and walk around in. Or sometimes we would pick up hot meals from the hospital and deliver them to older people who could no longer make it out of their houses. My grandfather and I did the kind of things you don't realize until you're much older that not everyone does.

At the end of a long day, we'd walk several blocks to the ice cream shop, the one with the old piano that played Ragtime tunes, mysteriously on its own, and the Elvis records and American flags and "I like Ike" metal buttons hung on the walls. We'd walk home with the sweet, creamy taste of strawberries and stories from our day's work on our lips.

One of my earliest memories is of my grandfather pulling me on a metal chute we used as a sled across the slab of concrete beside the garden behind his home; the metal against the concrete made a sound like plates of earth scraping against each other. And whenever I'd stay over on a school night, my grandpa would pack my lunch in an embarrassingly oversized, grocery-store paper bag, sending me off to school the next morning with a meal that was far too big for me to finish.

On the drive to school, he'd ask if I wanted to go to class or catch rabbits. My grandpa (who I called Bop, for reasons I cannot now remember) grew up in the South in the Dust Bowl era. The youngest boy in a family with too many mouths to feed and only his mother to raise them, he grew up learning how to catch his dinner. I don't think I ever traded school for catching rabbits. "I need to go to school," I'd tell my grandpa, and he'd say okay, put in a Ray Stevens cassette tape, and drive me to class.

As a boy, I dreamed about my future kids having two parents at home to tell them goodnight and never worrying about how the groceries were going to be paid for that month. And, perhaps naïvely, I figured if I worked really hard, harder than anyone else, I could form those dreams into a reality with my own two hands. That's what success looked like to me—always having fresh orange juice with breakfast, and a mom and a dad on the couch together for movie nights—even though I had no idea what it was I actually wanted to do with my life.

———————————— ❧ ————————————

Jen was standing on stage in our high school auditorium the first time I saw her. A tiara sat atop her neatly woven, chocolate-brown hair. She was dressed in a pink gown and was wearing the most beautiful smile I had ever seen. At a time when I needed a best friend, she became mine. It wasn't long after that I stood in our kitchen and told my mom that God had created that smile just for me. A few months later, I told Jen late one night that I loved her. And I did.

Like me, Jen was the oldest of three kids. But she had the kind of childhood I always dreamed of. Her dad coached her ball teams, and she was raised in a home where they went to church not just on Sundays, but on Wednesday nights, too. She grew up with a large extended family that spent their summers on the lake. She always knew she wanted to be a mother one day, and she knew she wanted to raise her kids with the same experiences she'd had as a young girl, surrounded by cousins and aunts and uncles and barbeques at the lake.

I wanted stability, and the money that would make it possible. Jen wanted a close family. At the time, I didn't realize just how different our dreams were. In a way, it's funny to think two kids who wanted such different things ended up together, but we did. Neither one of us would have guessed when I grafted my life to hers, and hers to mine, that we'd both leave our stable jobs and move to England just a few years into our marriage so I could study theology. But that's exactly what happened.

———————————— ❧ ————————————

Two classmates from middle school stand out in my mind to this day, largely because they helped shape much of the way I thought about religion for many years—about people who believe in God and those who laugh at people who do.

Even in middle school, Greg was the kid who always wanted to talk foreign policy and debate recent political news. He had a massive vocabulary, and he'd often use words that none of us knew. Greg spoke in a calm, dry tone most of the time. Except when he got worked up. Then his voice would quicken to a frantic pace.

Mindy sat in the front row at school and attended her church's youth group. She was polite, from a Christian home, and while I'm sure she made good grades, she wasn't known for her intelligence. Not like Greg.

Greg and Mindy's debates were renowned in our middle school. Their debates centered on Christianity, mostly, and the existence of God. Mindy stood on the side of belief and religion and Christianity. Greg represented those who thought such things were a joke. And Greg always steamrolled Mindy in these debates. She would often be so visibly frustrated by the time they were through that she'd only make the rest of us laugh even harder.

Though I didn't realize it until many years later, Greg and Mindy became caricatures in my mind of those who believe in God and those who do not. Believers, in my mind, were associated with Mindy: naïve and willing to accept ridiculous claims that no one in their right mind could actually believe. Those who cannot really explain why they should believe such things, but simply accept them because that's what they're supposed to do.

Nonbelievers, on the other hand, were associated in my mind with Greg: intellectual, rational, not accepting things on faith, but critically analyzing that which they believed before accepting it as true.

The unfortunate part about all of this is that I thought the Christian story was beautiful. My mom took me to church off and on growing up. I was even baptized when I was in the third grade, in that musty-scented church with the flannel board Jesus and the potlucks and the pastor's gray-haired wife who made the most delicious homemade applesauce. So I was familiar with the story of God entering our world to lay down his life, to make right not only the brokenness of our relationship with God, but the brokenness inside each one of us. It was the most extraordinary story I had ever heard. But I was still plagued by these caricatures. I was torn. I considered myself a relatively smart kid who could think for himself, and I didn't want people to think I was naïve. I knew there was a difference between thinking something is beautiful and thinking something is true. C. S. Lewis's writing made me think maybe Christianity could be both.

I remember reading Lewis's words on a late December night, by the light of my desk lamp in my grandparents' basement, where I lived as a college sophomore. I had never read Lewis before, so I knew very little about him. All I knew was that he wrote a few books about a lion and some children and a wardrobe (though I wasn't sure what a wardrobe was). But as I read Lewis's *Mere Christianity*, I suddenly realized this wasn't just a beautiful story. I realized Jesus was a real man, with real air in his real lungs, and real blood flowing through his real veins.

It sounds so funny to admit now, but Lewis's writing made me realize that maybe this beautiful story really did happen once. Maybe the veil was pulled back and we were all granted a glimpse of the unspeakable Mystery. Maybe the unspeakable really had become speakable; the untouchable, touchable. Most importantly, C. S. Lewis helped me realize Jesus' words had massive implications for my life.

In *Mere Christianity*, Lewis put his arm around my shoulder and said, "You don't have to feel like a fool for believing this, you know." That was the first time I ever felt that way. Lewis took a logical, creative approach to consider Christian beliefs. He used analogies and reason to talk about things like whether Christ was just a man or something more. And that approach was so foreign to me.

As I read his words, I found myself encouraged that I didn't have to leave my mind at the door in order to be a Christian. I felt like he pushed me to dig into the Christian faith in a way I never had before. Even though we never met, and even though he passed away more than twenty years before I was born, Lewis is the one who put my hand in the hand of our Lord and said with a smile, "Go for it, and don't feel as though you have to hold back."

"People don't realize how a man's whole life can be changed by one book," Malcolm X once wrote. And I think that's true. It's certainly true of my life. There in the dim stillness of my grandparents' basement, I put both feet into the Christian tradition for the first time. Lewis's words were encouraging me, pulling me along, inciting me to go the whole way to Christ and not look back. The Christian story became real to me that night in a way it never had before. Though I didn't realize it at the time, Lewis's words changed the entire direction of my life.

———————————— ✺ ————————————

After graduating from college and marrying Jen, I began working at a marketing and public relations firm. It was there that I discovered my passion for storytelling. One of my clients made braces for young girls and boys all over the world who had trouble walking because their legs and feet didn't work right. I loved sharing their stories.

Not all of my clients' stories were as admirable, of course. And it wasn't long before I began to imagine myself many years later looking back on my career and thinking, *This is what I did with my life: I helped companies make more money.*

It was also during this time that I realized Lewis's approach to questions about God and faith, about life in Christ had captured my heart. And my mind. Because of Lewis, I was reading and writing about theology in my free time. Before long, I realized I was the only person I knew who was working in public relations by day and reading and writing about theology by night. I began to wonder what that meant. Soon, I imagined a new path for my life. Or perhaps a new path was imagined for me; I'm not quite sure. But with a bit of education, I thought maybe I could help articulate the Christian narrative, the story of God's in-breaking Kingdom. Maybe I could write and speak in a way that helped make this Good News tangible, to help people feel its texture between their fingers, feel it in their bones. Perhaps I could even help others see Christ more clearly, as C. S. Lewis's writing had done for me.

I kept this idea to myself for some time before I finally shared it with my wife. I told Jen I felt God was calling me to use my gifts of writing and speaking to help tell his story. I also told her about my dream of going to Oxford to study theology. Even though Lewis never studied theology, that's where C. S. Lewis had studied and taught, and I knew I'd like to follow in his footsteps in some small way. Of course, this represented the complete opposite of Jen's dreams of staying near her family, of settling down and starting our own family. Without hesitating, she told me that she agreed. She thought God was calling me to this as well.

"You should at least apply," she told me. "That way you'll know if this is something we're supposed to do or not."

But I didn't. Not right away, at least. I was too scared.

Our good friends Doug and Carol were over for dinner a while after I first shared this thought with Jen. Doug and Carol are an older couple who have not only become close friends over the years, but also mentors in many ways. Carol is a bright, beautiful older woman with a singsong voice and attentive eyes. She is soft-spoken, and her warm presence feels like a plate of fresh-out-of-the-oven chocolate-chip cookies. Doug has a tall, athletic frame that spills the beans about his glory days as a basketball player. He's now a math professor; he taught Jen. Doug has a sharp, analytical mind, and we always have great conversations about faith and life whenever we're together.

The four of us were sitting around the living room, talking over coffee, after dinner at our home on this particular evening. Carol knew I had been talking with Doug about what I thought God might be calling us to do, about how I might integrate my faith with my work.

"So, where're you at with that, Ryan? What's the status of that itch?" Carol asked.

"Well, it's still there," I said, taken aback by her directness.

"Yeah? Well, what are you going to do about it?" she replied with a playful grin. She wasn't letting me off as easily as I had hoped.

"I don't know," I said with a shrug. "Nothing, probably."

Doug laughed from his seat across the room.

"Oh, come on!" Carol retorted. "What would you be doing if nothing was stopping you?"

I paused, to gauge if Carol really wanted to know, or if these questions were just for the sake of conversation. She looked back at me with narrowed eyes and a sly smile.

"If I could do anything? Honestly, I'd love to teach and write about theology someday."

"Really! Oh, Ryan, that would be great!" Carol paused for a moment, holding her coffee between her two hands and looking off somewhere in the corner of the room, letting this news settle in. Then she dove headfirst into making plans.

"Now, you'd have to go back to school. Where would you want to study?"

Again, I took a second to consider whether I should pour out my heart or hold at least part of it back.

I've gone this far, I thought to myself, *and she hasn't laughed me out of the room yet. I guess there's no hurt in going the rest of the way.* Even though this was totally out of my comfort zone, I decided to tell her.

"Oxford," I said. "I'd love to study at Oxford."

Carol's eyes got big and her mouth fell open.

"I knew it! I knew you were going to say that!"

"Really?" I asked, scrunching up my face.

"Yes, I just knew you'd want to go somewhere exceptional," she said. "I knew you'd want to travel and go somewhere far away."

Pausing once more, I could see her wheels turning. And then, looking at me with a smile, Carol finally spoke up.

"Well, you're going to have to go for it, then."

"Okay, but let's be realistic . . ."

"Realistic?!" Carol belted out so loudly and deliberately I was almost ashamed of my words. "What's not realistic about that, Ryan?"

Carol and Doug spent the next two hours talking Jen and me into booking a trip to England that summer. We would use the time to visit Oxford, to meet with professors, and to look into whether attending Oxford might even be an option.

"If you don't go after this now," Doug said from across the living room, finally breaking his silence, "you're going to spend the rest of your life wondering, what if?"

Doug was right. I knew I had no choice. This itch would not go away on its own.

After much prayer, many conversations, and our first trip to England, I applied to Oxford. But I never believed I'd actually get in. I knew I didn't fit the mold of the typical Oxford applicant—I wasn't even the valedictorian at my small, rural high school, and I was one of the first people in my family even to go to college. In fact, just confessing that I wanted to go to Oxford was embarrassing. But I applied, mostly so that I could sleep at night.

When I finally got up the courage to tell my grandfather what I was doing, he asked me where Oxford was.

"England," I told him.

"That's the worst news I've heard in a long time."

His words stung deeply. From as far back as I can remember, I only ever wanted to make my grandpa proud. Jen spoke up for me when I couldn't, explaining what an honor this would be if it actually came through. My grandpa was silent.

I spent three months working on applications and sitting through phone interviews. Even then, I was so sure I was not going to get in that it actually made things easier on me. The night before my phone interview, I found out only five people in the world had been accepted the year before to study theology at the college where I had applied. Only one of which was an American. In a weird way, knowing that being accepted was such a long shot erased any stress about the interviews. Jen and I were happy with our lives; we were certainly comfortable. We had great jobs, and we were surrounded by friends and family. We came to the conclusion that if I were accepted to Oxford, we'd go, and we'd pursue this calling that God had placed on my heart. And if I did not get in, well, we thought that must mean we were right where God wanted us.

"If it's where God wants you to be, it'll work out," my grandpa would eventually tell me.

On Christmas Eve, I received a letter in the mail. Were on our way to a Christmas party at the time and in such a hurry that I didn't even take the time to read the envelope, which would have told me it was from Oxford. Thankfully, I opened the letter before tossing it in the garbage with the rest of the junk mail. I was stunned to read the first sentence. Standing there in the kitchen in disbelief, all of our conversations and prayers and dreams about Oxford suddenly became a reality.

I made it to the living room, still holding the letter in my hand, just as Jen was coming down the stairs. Turning to look at me with those deep-blue eyes, she knew what had happened before I could say a word.

At twenty-five, I found myself saying good-bye to the kind of career I'd dreamed of as a young boy, worrying about things like rent and grocery bills and whether we'd stay in this house for more than a couple years. I was, of course, still the same little boy inside, lusting after a career that promised security for my family. And having no promise of security on the other side of this move scared me. Leaving a great job to go after what I believed God was calling me to felt irresponsible.

So I left my job with a cardboard bankers box in my hands and tears in my eyes, unsure of where this journey would lead us, but confident that this first step was the right one. Short of a calling that somehow came from beyond the two of us, there was no way Jen or I would have ever considered leaving behind all the comforts we enjoyed. We said good-bye to the only friends and family we had ever known, and I found myself sitting in an airport, staring out at the tarmac, waiting to board my flight to England. And it was there, waiting on this side of the Atlantic, that I found myself thinking, *This is going to change the rest of our lives. . . . What in the world have I done?*

2

Doubt

Arriving in Oxford

There are those rare moments in life when things slow down for a fleeting moment and you realize you are not some passive observer watching on as the story of your life passes by, but an active participant. Those moments when you think to yourself, *This is my life. This is not a dream. This is my life.* This was one of those moments.

"So, what brought you to Oxford?" asked a black-haired girl in thick-framed glasses. She was standing among a small group of British students while I awkwardly balanced a palm-sized plate of food, drink, and small talk, secretly wishing I could fade into the background of the dim room.

Arriving in Oxford felt like waking up in the middle of a *Harry Potter* film: foreign, out of place, and a bit magical. It was late September and my second night in the city when I found myself at a dinner party hosted by the Oxford theology faculty. In this fairy-tale world of castle-like cathedrals and English accents, I wondered if everyone else found my presence there strange, too.

"Lewis," I told them between bites, thinking my one-word response was self-explanatory. We were in Oxford, after all. The shared look of confusion on their faces told me it was not.

"Lewis?" the girl with glasses finally asked, her brow furrowed, exchanging sideways glances with the other students. "What does *Alice in Wonderland* have to do with theology?"

I was stunned. Before I arrived, I was half-expecting to find the city to be a shrine for the man who inspired me. As it turns out, it is not.

"Oh, no, I'm sorry. I meant *C. S.* Lewis, not Lewis Carroll," I said, explaining how Lewis's *Mere Christianity* had led me to want to study theology, leaving behind a career in marketing and public relations in the States.

"Ahhh . . ." the group breathed a collective sigh of understanding.

I noticed Rhona, my Greek professor who sounded eerily like Mrs. Doubtfire, standing in a corner of the room. She was snacking from her plate of food and eyeing the buzzing body of students with a smile. Seeing her there, my stomach felt heavy, as though I owed her a bit of an explanation.

I had arrived in Oxford the night before, a week before classes began, for preparatory Greek class with the rest of the first-year theology students. Along with introductions, our first class involved an exam in an old room just around the corner from where the original Hogwart's dining room was filmed. We were asked to complete several chapters of our Greek textbook before our first class, but in the midst of wrapping up my job back home and preparing to move, I had not completed all of my work before arriving. It showed when it came time for our first exam. I had finished long after everyone else, with lots of white space left on my paper. I handed it to Rhona with a sheepish grin.

I was not used to doing so poorly on an exam, and seeing Rhona standing there at the dinner party birthed a grapefruit-sized lump of guilt in the pit of my stomach. I wanted to assure her I was not nearly as dense as my exam suggested, and that I would work hard to catch up. So I did. As apologetically as I could, I tried to explain myself.

"Don't worry, Ryan," she encouraged me in her grandmother-like English accent, which rang like a bell on the high notes. "You'll catch up, I'm sure of it."

Her eyes seemed to twinkle behind her glasses as she smiled at me. I breathed a sigh of relief and thanked her. She asked about what had brought me to Oxford. And this time I made sure to qualify my "Lewis" explanation with his first initials.

"How wonderful," she said, her eyes now beaming. "I am very fond of his writing. Do you know, one of my former students lived in his home last year?"

Rhona went on to tell me about how this student had invited her over for tea at C. S. Lewis's former home, and how she had not yet been able to take him up on the offer.

"He's still here in Oxford, though I don't know whether he's still living there. Perhaps I could write and see if we could both join him for tea there, if you'd like?"

I had not yet been in Oxford for a full twenty-four hours and I had already received an invitation to tea at C. S. Lewis's home. I stood there dumbfounded, staring back at Rhona for what could have been several seconds.

"Yes, yes, sorry. Yes, of course. I would like that very much!"

Called

———————— ❧ ————————

"Okay, great. Let's get one with your cap on now, shall we?" Jane asked in her posh British accent as we stood in the half-moon gravel driveway in front of her North Oxford home.

Jane and her husband, Justin, owned the mansion of a home that loomed behind where we stood. I was staying in the small mother-in-law suite attached to the side of the house. She was taking photos of me in my cap and gown before my matriculation ceremony, where I would become an official member of Oxford University. Jane was kind enough to snap a few photos for me to share with family back home, and I felt like a high school kid again, taking prom photos with my mom before picking up my date.

Both Jane and Justin are Oxford alums. They have two sons. Daniel was away at boarding school most days; Felix, the younger of the two, attended a nearby prep school and was often carrying either a rugby ball under his arm or a cricket bat on his shoulder.

Meeting their family made my arrival in Oxford seem even more surreal. I soon discovered that Justin co-owns several newspapers in London, and that the couple frequently attended parties with the kind of people most folks only read about. One evening, I stayed with Felix while Justin and Jane attended a party at Sir Elton John's house. I was told that J. K. Rowling, Hugh Grant, and Kevin Spacey would be there.

"Ask her if she's going to write any more *Harry Potter* books when you see her, Dad," Felix begged his father in an excited voice before they left that evening.

I loved living there, in the annex attached to Jane and Justin's home. I loved everything about it. Well, everything except the recycling system. I've never seen such an intricate recycling system, and I come from the Pacific Northwest, where we recycle our recycling. Navigating the six different color-coded recycling bins was nearly as confusing as the Greek I was learning. Every so often I'd get it wrong, and Jane would not-so-subtly slip another copy of the fifteen-page, color-coded recycling guide under my door. Or she would stop me in the hallway and ask if I had not read the guides she'd given me, before asking Beng, the family's black-haired Filipino maid with a thick-as-mud accent, to go over the routine with me once again. Each time, I was sure Jane, Justin, and Beng were all laughing to themselves, wondering how I ever managed to sneak my way into Oxford.

Jane snapped several more photos of me in my dark cap and gown in the late-morning sun before I left for the matriculation ceremony. Before I left, Jane asked if I knew the house across the street was where *The Lord of The Rings* had been written.

Sure enough, a small blue plaque hung at the top of the house's peak, with J. R. R. Tolkien's name and the dates he had lived there scrolled in white letters. I thanked Jane for the photos, taking her off guard with my hug, and I made my way to the university's matriculation ceremony, smiling at the plaque on the home across the street as I went.

———————— ❧ ————————

I'm told that when C. S. Lewis used to lecture, students would regularly pack out the lecture hall. Bikes would be stacked five rows deep outside the building by those hoping to get a chance to hear him. Apparently he would start lecturing just before he entered the room, and he'd only finish while making his exit, his Oxford robes flapping behind him as he left.

Perhaps the closest I came to experiencing a Lewis-like lecture was with a patristics professor by the name of Mark Edwards. He is, in every meaning of the word, brilliant. He also epitomizes Oxford. Professor Edwards entered the lecture hall dressed in a button-up shirt, tie, sweater (with a stain from breakfast on the belly), scarf, tweed jacket, black academic gown, and glasses, slightly askew. His hair was messy, his face scruffy.

His gown flowed behind him as he entered the lecture hall and made his way to the front of the room just as the minute hand reached the top of the hour. He poured himself a glass of water (which he held for the entirety of class), and then he immediately began to lecture. Fast. And nonstop, for a full hour. No pauses. Straight through. He spit out names and dates with ease, making smooth transitions throughout.

And then, an hour later on the dot: "Next week I shall talk about the Gnostics."

He drank the glass of water he had been holding in one long swallow, set it down, and was out the door before anyone could move.

I continued to struggle through Greek, doing my best to catch up on the reading I hadn't finished before arriving, as well as to learn what Rhona was currently teaching. I groaned at the start of every morning, knowing another Greek quiz awaited me. I was not used to being the student who struggled to keep up, but at Oxford I was forced to swallow my pride and ask for the help of a private tutor so I could keep up with my classmates. It felt like admitting failure, but it was the only thing that kept me from slipping even further behind.

Adjusting to life in a foreign country was also harder than I assumed it would be. I figured living in England wouldn't be much different from living in the States, which only made adjusting to the differences that much harder. English keyboards had a foreign layout, which made typing a chore. And there were the switches that had to be turned on before you could use an electric outlet, which I always forgot to flip. Of course, none of my American electronics actually fit any of the outlets, which doesn't sound like a big deal, but I can't tell you how many times I wanted to simply plug in my laptop without needing to make sure I had the right adaptor on me.

I mentioned these frustrations to Dave, my New Testament tutor (and a fellow American), a few weeks after I arrived. He smiled knowingly, and shared with me something someone had told him when he first arrived.

"It's a bit like returning to your home and finding everything moved clockwise ninety degrees," he said. "Everything's familiar, but you know something's not quite right."

I had been on my own for the first couple of weeks in Oxford. Because of visa problems, Jen had to remain in the States for a few extra weeks while I began school. This didn't make my adjustment any easier. On top of getting used to life in a foreign country and trying to keep up with my studies, I often found myself missing my wife deeply.

We had been married for four years before we set out for Oxford, which is a lot of nights falling asleep and waking up with her breath falling softly on the pillow next to mine. I would crawl into bed alone after long days of working at the library, just wishing she were there with me. I'd call her during the early morning hours, and she'd listen patiently.

"I don't know if I can keep at it," I'd tell her through tears. "I've been thinking about writing my old office to tell them I've made a big mistake and asking for my job back."

I'd tell Jen I was pretty sure I didn't need to learn koiné Greek to become a writer. And then, after she had listened patiently, she would tell me to keep going.

"It's only been a couple weeks, Ryan," she'd say in a calm, collected voice. "I know it's been difficult trying to learn Greek with so many changes. And I know it's tough being apart. It's tough on me, too. But we'll be together again soon.

"Besides, you know this is where God has called you. Keep at it, hon. Keep going."

Jen has always been tougher than I am.

———————— ❧ ————————

"What do you do to relax?" I asked Emily, a classmate, one afternoon. "I mean, what do you do to give yourself a break from all of these studies?"

We had just left our Greek tutorial with Rhona in Christ Church, and we were walking through the college courtyard, a green lawn surrounded by the high, stone college walls, with a fountain statue of the Greek god Mercury in the center. Emily grew up in a small town just thirty minutes south of Oxford. She has dark-brown eyes that match her hair, and she was one of the few English students I found willing to admit to feeling overwhelmed.

"Honestly?" she began. "Staying on top of my work relaxes me. When I get behind, that's when I get stressed." Her answer was more studious than I had expected, which made me feel a bit insecure.

"What about you?" she asked, turning her head to face me as we walked.

"Me? Uh, well . . . writing, I guess."

"Writing? You relax from school by writing?"

"Yeah, I guess I do. I find it therapeutic. It helps me think. It helps me interpret things. Like what I'm doing, and why I'm here."

She nodded as though she understood my explanation, even though I could see how confusing it must have sounded.

Admitting this to Emily felt strange. It made me feel naked. Writing had been a big part of my life before I arrived in Oxford. In a way, writing was what brought me to Oxford. But I also came to Oxford reluctant to share my dreams of writing with anyone. It would take some time, and a series of dramatic experiences, for that to change.

I was in my mid-twenties when I began writing for therapy, after writing for clients all day. But my relationship with words started much earlier. It began with a fascination that I could not ignore. When I was a young boy, I would get words stuck in my head, just swirling around. I would spell them out, letter by letter, until I knew them backward and forward.

"O-N-I-O-N." The first word I ever learned to spell. My mother taught me, putting it to a rhyme. "O-N." Pause. And then, as quickly as I could, "I-O-N." I wrote it in ink several times on a piece of paper, folded it neatly, and then hid it under our house for whoever might find my mysterious note years later.

"T-U-M-B-L-E-W-E-E-D." The word was painted in giant, uppercase letters on the side of the corner store, down the street from my grandfather's house. "M-A-R-K-E-T." I didn't know what a tumbleweed was, and I wondered what it had to do with a market, but I spelled it until I couldn't get it out of my head. And then for a while after that.

I liked how certain words felt on my tongue. "Scratch." And how I had to move my lips around others. "Peaches." I liked how particular words could take you places. Places you'd never been before; places you longed to return to.

My mom is the only one I ever admitted my obsession with words to. I told her how frustrating it was at times, and how I wished I could stop. She told me it was good for me.

The fact that Oxford has thirty-eight different colleges can be a bit confusing for those unfamiliar with the Oxford system. Every Oxford student is a member of a particular college, and together these colleges make up Oxford University. Harris Manchester College, a smallish college nestled off the beaten path of the city's busier streets, is where I attended.

Harris Manchester hosted a meet-and-greet for the college's theology students before the start of the term, so that new students could meet their tutors and classmates. It was there that I met Cole, one of only two other Americans in the program. Cole wore glasses, long hair, and what seemed to be a permanent grin on his round face. He had a great laugh that shook his whole body.

When I told him my interest in C. S. Lewis's writing brought me to Oxford, Cole appeared overjoyed. He told me he was a Lewis fan himself, and that he was the vice president of the Oxford University C. S. Lewis Society. He went on to tell me he spent his first year in Oxford living in Lewis's old home; Cole was the student Rhona had told me about.

Though neither of us realized it at the time, Cole would become one of my closest friends in Oxford. He would introduce me to the world of C. S. Lewis in this old city, and we would soon be sharing tea together during my first visit to the Kilns, Lewis's former home.

I celebrated the end of my first week of studies with Cole at an old pub called The Eagle & Child. Long before I arrived in Oxford, I had read about The Eagle & Child as the famous meeting place for the Inklings. The Inklings was the literary group founded by C. S. Lewis; J. R. R. Tolkien; Lewis's brother, Warnie; their friends Owen Barfield, Charles Williams, Hugo Dyson; and others. The group met at the pub each week to chat over pints and pipes, and even to share their work with each other from time to time. Stories from *The Chronicles of Narnia* and *The Lord of the Rings* would have been shared with this group before readers around the world were introduced to them.

Cole greeted me under the street lamp at the front of the pub.

"Heyyy!" he said, wrapping me in a tight hug. "You did it! How does it feel to have your first week as an Oxford student behind you?"

"Completely unreal," I confessed in a voice that revealed my exhaustion.

Cole laughed loudly. "Good, good," he said, patting me on the back. "Well, come on in. It's about to feel even more unreal."

Cole pulled open the thick, wood door and took a step inside. I followed, ducking under the low door frame. We entered a dimly lit, narrow room with low ceilings. Pocket-sized rooms revealing people sitting at small tables were tucked on either side.

The air was thick with the smell of ale that had been soaking into the hardwood bar counter for centuries. Packed though it was, I found myself feeling embraced by the cramped pub. Like a hug from an old friend.

We placed our order at the bar with a man who knew Cole by name, then took our seats at a table in one of the small rooms at the front of the restaurant. Cole told me about his life in the States before Oxford as we waited on our food to arrive, his studies in New York, and his dreams of being an actor. I was not surprised. Cole sounded like a character in a medieval story about knights and dragons and lessons of chivalry when he spoke. His voice had a tone of excitement and he used words of grandeur. Cole went on to tell me about his dreams of opening his own theatre house, where he would perform scripts that explored Christian themes in the hopes of creating thoughtful questions and conversation.

Our food arrived a few minutes later. We continued sharing stories between bites. Cole told me about being out for dinner with his dad when he received the news that he had been accepted to Oxford: "He pulled the waitress aside and said, 'My son's just been accepted to Oxford!'"

Cole's face reflected his father's pride. Lewis, Tolkien, and others smiled down on us from photos on the walls.

"So we're on for tea at the Kilns," Cole said with a look of accomplishment. Rhona had written him shortly after she and I met, and Cole had quickly taken care of the arrangements. "You'll be joining me, Rhona, and her husband, the dean of Christ Church. It'll be great."

A couple nights earlier, the principal of our college welcomed the first-year students to Oxford. He talked about the incredible honor it was to be part of this community, both the college and the university. He told us our time there would require a lot of hard work, but that we should not lose sight of where we were. He talked about how the university had denied twenty thousand applications that year, and how hundreds of thousands of others around the world who didn't apply would love to be in our shoes. He talked about the great men and women who had attended both the college and the university before us, and he mentioned their contributions to the world. It all had left me feeling as though I was in the wrong place.

Two weeks earlier I was still working in a marketing firm back home. Now, I was a student at Oxford, and in just a couple weeks' time, I'd be having tea at C. S. Lewis's old home with the dean of the most influential college at Oxford.

"I have to tell you, Cole, this doesn't feel quite right. My being here, I mean," I confessed, taking a break from my meat pie. "I keep feeling like someone is going to realize there's been some sort of a mistake and I'm going to have to go home."

Cole eyed me with a grin and a nod.

"Impostor syndrome," Cole said as though he were diagnosing a head cold. I gave him a blank look.

He told me his mom is a doctor who teaches medical students in Virginia. She had told Cole at one point about how her medical students often struggled with the same feeling: they believe that the only reason they were accepted to medical school was because someone made a mistake, and that they would be sent home just as soon as the med-school administration found out. Secretly, they go through school with this self-doubt wrecking their insides.

Apparently students aren't the only ones who struggle with these anxieties. Cole told me that even people with years of experience in their fields, at whom others look and think, "This person's really made it," struggle with the same fears of being found out.

"Ryan, you've matriculated," Cole said. "You're now an official member of the University of Oxford, and you will be for the rest of your life."

Cole's eyes were now genuinely beaming with pride.

"You are just as much a member of the university as the professors."

I thanked Cole, with a half-hearted smile. Despite his words, I couldn't shake the feeling that someone had made a mistake somewhere along the way.

At times, Oxford can seem more like a postcard than real life. This was particularly true in autumn.

The neighborhood where we lived in North Oxford was leafy, with tall trees that shed their crisp burnt-orange and brown clothes in the autumn, covering the sidewalk until they were crunched underfoot. Children streamed the narrow lanes in their private-school outfits. Little girls in skirts and sweater vests ran and laughed. Boys in suits and shorts with knee-high socks played tag as they were let out of school. Parents in BMWs, Volvos, and Mercedes parked along the curb, waiting to pick up their kids.

Cycling home through such scenes, I'd often wish I could pull it all together into a single picture, place it on a postcard, and share it with everyone back home.

As relentless as my study schedule was, I kept thinking how much there was I wanted to share with Jen. I did my best to do so over Skype, but it just wasn't the same without her there. When she finally did arrive, nearly a month into my term, I couldn't stop smiling. I was thrilled to be together again, in our new home. But this transition was not without its challenges.

My daily routine at Oxford involved spending long days in the library, working through a pile of books and then hurrying to finish an essay before tutorial. When the library closed, I'd study Greek flash cards at home until I could no longer keep my eyes open, which usually came around two o'clock in the morning. A few hours later, I'd pull myself out of bed to do it all over again. Jen, on the other hand, faced an empty schedule for the first time in years. She struggled to transition from being involved in everything from coaching volleyball to helping out at our church's youth group, to starting over in a place where she didn't know anyone. She missed her family and friends back home. Though Jen is easily the toughest member of our marriage, as incredible as Oxford is, it wasn't home, and Jen was painfully aware of that.

"I know I should get out and explore," she'd tell me late at night, "but I don't have anyone here to do that with. Going out only reminds me how alone I feel."

I hated spending so much time away from Jen. I knew how much she was struggling with this move, but I also knew what it would take just to keep up with school. I would come home at night after a marathon of books and essays, look into her eyes and feel sick with guilt for putting her through all of this. I began to wonder if being at Oxford was worth it. Even worse, I wondered if we had even been called here at all.

Was it Your voice I heard? I would ask. *Or was this just the voice of my pride? My ego?*

Yet it was Jen who encouraged me to keep going when I doubted God's call. It was Jen who reassured me that Oxford was precisely where we were supposed to be, and that the Lord was leading us in all of this.

But missing friends and family back home and struggling to settle into our new life in Oxford was just the beginning. The spring before we left for England, Jen's parents received a phone call late one evening. It was the local hospital. The voice on the other end of the line told them to come quickly. Jen's youngest sister, Hayley, had been dropped off in front of the hospital. She was not breathing and her heart had stopped.

Hayley was ten years old, with curly hair, awkward glasses, and a mischievous grin, when we first met. After Jen and I were married, Hayley never called me her brother-in-law; I was always simply her brother.

Jen's family had me over for dinner shortly after we began dating. I was pretty quiet during the meal, still a bit shy, and wanting to make a good impression. Hayley didn't say a word. But then, while we were all sitting around the table talking and joking after we had finished eating, I spoke up to say something, and Hayley immediately cut me off.

"You're doing this," she said, making her hand into a mouth and moving it as if it were talking, "and I want you to do this," she continued, closing her hand-mouth.

We were all stunned. There were several seconds of silence before we burst into laughter.

In the early morning hours the day after she was dropped off at the hospital, a doctor spoke plainly to our family in the ICU waiting room.

"She's breathing again," he told us, "thanks to the help of a life-support machine we have her on. But there's still a lot of work to be done. We need to make sure her brain function is restored. At the moment, she's not responding."

Several months before receiving this news, Jen's parents; her sister, Leann, and her husband; Hayley; and Jen and I had gathered together at her grandparents' house on Christmas Eve. With wrapping paper and presents strewn across the room and the tree all lit up, Hayley tried to persuade me that she could carry me. I had laughed in response, and told her she was crazy.

"I have sixty, seventy pounds on you. At least."

"So? I can carry you. Watch."

When I finally gave in, Hayley not only held my weight, her tiny frame carried me across the room. Jen smiled and shook her head as she watched from her grandmother's couch.

We sat beside Hayley's hospital bed for five days after her parents first received that phone call, praying, brushing her hair, cradling her cold hands in ours. When it was just her and Hayley in the room, Jen sang to her. Leann, their middle-sister, washed and styled Hayley's hair, just like before prom. All of us held out hope that our sister would be able to come home. We prayed over and over that we'd all be able to leave the sanitized rooms and linens behind. Our church prayed alongside us, as did most of our community, which flooded the halls of the hospital, waiting for good news. But that good news never came. Those cold hands never got warm.

At the end of that week, we were led into a small office that felt like a broom closet, where a neurosurgeon told us in a robotic voice that Hayley would not get better. We sat there, dumbfounded, as if suspended in time. I remember leaving that cramped room, walking down a long hallway that smelled like floor cleaner, and stopping to stare out a window at cotton-ball clouds floating by in the pale blue sky. For the first time in my life, I had no idea what to pray for.

The next day, our family held Hayley's cold hands and prayed and sang songs and cried—my God, did we cry. At 11:06 that evening, we watched as Hayley struggled like a fish out of water to breathe her final breath. And then, she was gone. I have never seen anyone look so confused as Jen's parents did that evening.

We said good-bye to Hayley when she was just nineteen years old, and we left for Oxford with hearts still shattered, struggling to put together the pieces some six thousand miles away from the only community we had ever known.

Jen and I were walking home late one evening in Oxford when I was wrestling with doubt. I wondered aloud whether we had made the wrong decision in coming to England and whether this was where we were actually called. It was then that Jen mentioned Hayley, which neither one of us often did. The wound was still too fresh.

"Hayley believed in this, you know?" Jen reminded me as we walked along the sidewalk in the dark, our jackets pulled up to our cheeks in the cold night air. She paused. Her eyes took on a glossy sheen.

Jen was referring to a text message Hayley had sent me shortly before her death, not long after she found out I had been accepted to Oxford. Hayley had been reading my writing before bed at night, in a little book that my best friend, Steve, had published for me as a birthday present. She knew my writing had to do with why we were leaving.

"You're going to impact a lot of people's lives," Hayley's last text message read. "You have mine."

"She believed in you and your writing," Jen continued, now looking at me as we walked under the streetlamps in north Oxford. "It made a difference in her life. I don't think that's *why* she's gone, but maybe God knew you'd need those words."

3

Dreams

Tea at C. S. Lewis's Home

The Oxford University C. S. Lewis Society invites scholars from around the world to speak to members at its Tuesday-night meetings about figures like C. S. Lewis and J. R. R. Tolkien, as well as those who had an influence on the group known as the Inklings, such as G. K. Chesterton and George MacDonald. While I had more work than I knew what to do with, between my Old Testament and New Testament tutorials, not to mention learning Greek, I decided to check out the Society's meeting one Tuesday evening early in the term. I figured it would be a healthy break from my relentless study schedule.

I was taken aback to find that the speaker for the evening was an American, a professor from Wheaton College by the name of Chris Mitchell. He oversaw the largest collection of C. S. Lewis literature in the world, which was housed at Wheaton.

That evening, Chris spoke about C. S. Lewis and his impact on historical evangelism to a group of thirty or so people packed into a tight room. He talked about how Lewis's influence has touched the lives of those from a wide variety of Christian traditions. Chris emphasized that Lewis's focus was on *mere* Christianity, on the core of the faith, rather than the differences between denominations.

Chris went on to explain that Lewis's writings on Christianity were not well received by many of his Oxford colleagues. He told us Lewis was often shunned by Oxford dons who didn't think it was proper to share your religious views, or to write on a topic so clearly outside of your expertise (Lewis's academic background was medieval literature). The reason Lewis did so, Chris explained, was because he believed it was his duty, even though he knew it risked harming his own reputation, particularly in academic circles. Lewis believed it was every Christian's responsibility to use the resources they have been given to help spread the Good News of God's in-breaking Kingdom. Lewis knew he had been gifted with an exceptional education and the ability to teach and write. So he did.

"Lewis was a real lover of souls," Chris said with a smile.

Sitting there listening to Chris, I began to think there was a lesson there. We may not all be gifted with the same intellect or literary talents as C. S. Lewis, but we've all been gifted in one way or another. Chris's point reminded me of a trip I took to Maine one spring break when I was a senior in college. Along with Jen and twenty other students, I visited a small house nestled among snow-blanketed fields. The house was on a long, gravel road that stretched into the secluded woods. It was built as a shelter for women and children who had decided to leave their abusive homes, and it was our job to help with repairs on the house. We spent several days that week painting and cleaning.

Before we got there, all the work was left to one guy: Doug. Doug had long, dark hair, which he wore in a ponytail. He wore jeans and a hooded sweatshirt and often had a cup of coffee in his hand. I remember one lunch break someone asked Doug why he volunteered his time repairing this house when there were so many other things he could be doing. The simplicity of his response surprised me.

"Because I can," he said, nonchalantly, taking a sip from his coffee mug. That was it. Not because of some life-changing experience that allowed him to sympathize with these mothers and children. Not because he was serving time for something he had done. But because he had two hands and a bit of experience with a hammer.

Doug used his hands to build homes for women and children whose husbands and fathers used their hands to beat them. Lewis used his hands and a pen to create worlds for others to enter, or to think through their faith. I think that's what we are all meant to do, all we can do, with the gifts we have been given, be they experiences or talents. Those gifts are waiting to be used to touch others' lives, as we patiently listen for and obediently follow the direction to which God is calling us. Because that's what you do with gifts, you give them away.

After Chris finished his talk that evening, one of the guests in the audience raised his hand and asked about Lewis's position on reformed theology versus evangelism. Before Chris could respond, another man in the room spoke up. He was an older man by the name of Walter Hooper. He had known C. S. Lewis personally.

Walter had thick glasses and his white hair was slicked back across his head. He wore a tweed jacket with a V-neck sweater that revealed a dress shirt and tie underneath. Walter had been Lewis's personal secretary toward the end of Lewis's life, when his health was in poor shape. He was now an advisor to Lewis's literary estate.

"I remember standing just down the street from here, on Cornmarket Street," Walter spoke up. "And I remember Jack saying [Lewis went by 'Jack' with all his close friends], 'Imagine a spaceship landing right here before us and a group of Martians walking out and greeting us. Imagine they say to us, *Now we only have a few minutes before we have to return to Mars, so please don't mind our frightful appearance. We hear you have some Good News. We would very much like to hear this before returning home. Can you tell us about it?*

"'And you know what would happen, don't you? Surely someone would speak up and say, *Well yes, this church over here, they have liturgy, but the other church in town does not. And that church over there, they have candles, but the first church I told you about, they do not* . . . And what would happen? Well, the Martians would return home having not heard the Good News.'

"The point of all this," Walter explained, "is that Lewis believed we are far more concerned with church format and denominational differences than we should be. What we should be concerned about is the real matter before us: sharing the Good News."

I smiled at Walter's story from my seat at the rear of the room. Hearing about Lewis's commitment to helping others better understand their Christian faith, even at the risk of his reputation, made me appreciation his work even more. It also made me think seriously about the gifts I had been given. It made me want to write in a way that might help others, in my own day.

Still grinning when I caught up with Cole afterward, I thanked him for introducing me to the Society, and told him that I was so glad I came. I mentioned how much I loved hearing Walter's story, and that I'd appreciate meeting him at some point. So he introduced me, right then and there.

"He's such a kind man," Cole assured me, taking off toward the front of the room before I realized what he was doing.

"Hi, Walter, I have a friend here I'd like you to meet," Cole said, speaking to Walter. "This is Ryan. He's just arrived here in Oxford. He's studying at my college and he's a big fan of Lewis."

I thanked Cole, and I explained to Walter that Lewis's writing made me want to come to Oxford.

"How wonderful," Walter said with a soft voice and wide smile.

We talked a bit more, and Walter took out a small notebook from his jacket pocket. He wrote my name on a page and slid it back into his coat pocket. Walter asked where I was living, and I told him.

"Is that so? Well you know I live not far from there. You must come over for tea sometime."

"I'd like that a lot."

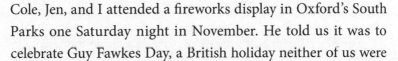

Cole, Jen, and I attended a fireworks display in Oxford's South Parks one Saturday night in November. He told us it was to celebrate Guy Fawkes Day, a British holiday neither of us were familiar with.

In something of an informal history lesson, Cole told us that Guy Fawkes was a man who made plans to blow up parliament a few hundred years ago, and how he was discovered and thwarted at the last minute. He told us the British still celebrate catching

Guy Fawkes to this day by lighting giant wooden effigies of him on fire each year, all around the country. They top the whole thing off with a fireworks display.

It was dark when we made it to the park, along with hundreds of other people, all funneling through a small iron gate. The ground was covered in straw and the park was filled with the sweet, salty smell of fried food as carnival rides lit up the night sky with neon bulbs and children's laughter. It felt like we had walked into a county fair.

We settled on hot pork sandwiches for dinner and found a spot in the crowd to enjoy the show. The air was cold and steam rose upward, pouring out from our sandwiches. It wasn't long before the fireworks began. The crowd was gathered together tightly. Everyone's heads were craned upward, taking in the show.

I looked over at Cole about halfway through the fireworks and asked him how much he'd give me to start singing, "God Bless America." He laughed, and he told me he'd give me a pat on the back. I decided against it, figuring I didn't need an effigy in my honor.

The fireworks really were beautiful, though. And I found myself remembering something I had read a few days before, a quote from a British journalist named Matthew Parris, a professed atheist.

> The New Testament offers a picture of a God who does not sound at all vague to me. He has sent his son to Earth. He has distinct plans both for his son and for mankind. He knows each of us personally and can communicate directly with us. We are capable of forming a direct relationship, individually with him,

and are commanded to try. We are told this can be done only through his son. And we are offered the prospect of eternal life—an afterlife of happy, blissful, or glorious circumstances. . . .

Friends, if I believe that, or even a tenth of that . . . I would drop my job, sell my house, throw away my possessions, leave my acquaintances and set out into the world burning with the desire to know more and, when I had found out more, to act upon it and tell others.[1]

As I watched the fireworks light up the black canopy overhead with bright whites and blues and reds and oranges, I found myself thinking about the kind of Christianity the atheist Matthew Parris had described. Watching the fireworks explode in a bouquet of colors, I thought how beautiful that kind of Christian faith would be. Like fireworks, it would stand out. I think it would be so captivating that people would stop to take it in when they heard about it. When they had seen it for themselves, I think they'd tell their friends. And, as they closed their eyes to go to bed at night, I think the scene would play again before the darks of their eyelids. They'd fall asleep with a smile on their face, thinking about how beautiful it was. Just like fireworks.

—————————————— ❦ ——————————————

"This must be us," Jen said, spotting the sign before Steve or I saw it.

Steve, my best friend from back home, was visiting at the time. I was thrilled to be able to bring him and Jen along for tea at C. S. Lewis's former home. We took a bus from the Oxford city center to the small village called Risinghurst. The bus went up a steep hill by the park where Cole, Jen, and I watched the fireworks on Guy Fawkes Day. We rode through a small town, circled a roundabout, and, finally, made our way up a low-sloping hill that led to a small road called "Lewis Close."

"Hey, yeah, there it is!" I said, tugging the bus cord that signaled our stop.

I had met Steve at a friend's birthday party years earlier, and it wasn't long before he asked me what my dreams were. His question caught me off guard, so much so that I let it slip about my dreams of writing and studying at Oxford before I could stop myself. He was only the second person I admitted this to, after Jen. Since that night, he had played a major role in my coming to Oxford, even when it meant the inevitable good-bye.

The three of us got off the bus and made the short walk down the lane before spotting a small cottage nestled behind a row of birch trees, bordering a forest and hill that extended into the sky beyond it.

"I think that's it," I said as we came around the front of the house. "I think that's Lewis's old home."

I spotted a blue plaque at the peak of the roof. It was similar to the plaque on Tolkien's home, and it had Lewis's name on it: "C. S. Lewis, 1898–1963. Scholar and author, lived here 1930–1963."

I was still reading the plaque when a cab pulled up. The back door opened and Walter Hooper stepped out onto the street, not far from where we were standing.

"Walter, hi, it's Ryan Pemberton," I said, making my way over to where he was standing and offering my hand for a shake. "We met at the Society meeting the other night."

"Well, hello, Ryan. Yes, of course, I remember you. Will you be joining us for today's tea?"

"I am, yeah. I didn't realize you were coming."

Walter told me Cole had invited him, and I introduced him to Jen and Steve. He greeted them each before reaching into his coat pocket and pulling out a small journal. The same one he had written in when I first met him.

"I'm just going to put your names down here," he said. "And look who that is!" He opened the page to my name.

"Hey, you made it!" Cole's voice rang out as we saw him round the front of the house and make his way to us.

Cole had arrived early to help Debbie prepare the afternoon's tea. Debbie managed the house, which was owned by the C. S. Lewis Foundation, a nonprofit from California.

"I've been preparing cucumber sandwiches and scones all morning," Cole told us, wiping his hands on his jeans. "Debbie put me to work straight away!"

Just then, Rhona and her husband arrived on their bikes. They were wearing their helmets and breathing heavy from the ride.

"Hullo," Rhona said, greeting the small crowd now gathered in the street.

"Rhona, Chris, hello!" Cole said. "So glad you both could join us. Well, it looks like we're all here. Let's go inside, shall we?"

Cole led us inside and Walter began telling us about the home. He said he had lived there for several years with Lewis's brother, Major Warren Lewis, or Warnie, as he was called, after Lewis passed away. Walter told us that Lewis had first moved into the house not with his brother, but with two women—Mrs.

Moore and her daughter, Maureen—after an interesting turn of events.

Lewis first arrived in Oxford preparing to enter the university as a student during World War I—or The Great War, as it was then called. An Irishman by birth, Lewis was not required to enlist, but he felt it was his duty. Walter told us that Lewis bunked with a fellow by the name of Paddy Moore. Before leaving for the war, the two men became friends and they soon realized they had something important in common: Lewis had lost his mother before his tenth birthday, and Paddy's father had also passed away. Knowing this, the two men made a pact: if one of them did not return from the war, the other would look after that man's family.

The two men left for the First World War with this promise to each other. Walter told us that Lewis was hit by a piece of shrapnel, which sent him to the hospital and away from the enemy lines. Lewis's friend Paddy wasn't so lucky; he didn't return alive. Lewis kept his vow and he moved in with Paddy's mother and sister when he finally returned to Oxford. The three of them lived in several homes in Oxfordshire while Lewis finished his studies, before moving into the Kilns in 1930, after Lewis had begun to teach at Oxford. A couple years later, after retiring from the military, Lewis's brother Warnie also moved into the home. Though they had some difficult years, Warnie was Lewis's oldest friend; this arrangement pleased him very much. Between Mrs. Moore's savings and the Lewis brothers' inheritance from the sale of their childhood home in Belfast (their father, Albert Lewis, died the year before Lewis moved into the Kilns), they bought the home and eight acres of undeveloped property where Lewis would spend the next 30 years of his life for just £3,300, or around $5,000. Tolkien had encouraged Lewis to buy the property next to the house for an additional £500, but he insisted that was far too much money.

Unlike most of his Oxford colleagues, Lewis's life involved many domestic responsibilities. It's only been within the past 100 years or so that Oxford Professors have even been able to live out of college. Prior to that time, it was expected that those teaching at the University lived something of a monastic life-style, focusing on their research, writing, and teaching behind college walls. All of their meals and rooms were provided in college, which made for an ivory tower sort of lifestyle, removed from the chores and duties common to most lifestyles. Which made Lewis's experience of washing dishes and taking care of animals around the house unique. He even looked after Mrs. Moore in her old age, until around 1950, when she was moved to a nursing home in North Oxford. Lewis visited her there every day, we were told, until she passed away. Maureen, Mrs. Moore's daughter, became like the sister Lewis had never had growing up, and they remained close long after she got married and moved out. When Maureen passed away in the 1990s, several pieces of Lewis's writings were read at her service, per her request.

The home where they lived was known as the Kilns, Walter explained, because there used to stand beside the house two large brick kilns that didn't come down until after C. S. Lewis passed away, in the 1960s. Before Lewis got there, these kilns were used to fire bricks from clay dredged from the pond that sat at the base of the hill, just beyond the house.

"The home wasn't built to be anything special," Walter told us. "Just to house these stone workers, you see."

In fact, Lewis hadn't even set foot inside the house before he bought it. He loved the area so much—for its seclusion, its woods, and the animals that roamed there—that he didn't need to look inside. It had everything he wanted.

After a bit of background on Lewis's arrival at the Kilns, Walter showed us around the inside of the home, taking care to point out pictures and objects of note along the way. We began in Lewis's front room, which Walter referred to as the "common room." One side of the wall was covered in bookshelves, from floor to ceiling. A couch sat against the opposite wall. Beneath the window that looked out over the front garden was a desk. Though this particular desk was not original to the home, Walter told us that Lewis would have enjoyed the view of the garden and woods surrounding the pond as he worked from the desk that originally sat there, looking out through the window in the front room.

Walter told us Lewis and Warnie would often entertain their friends in this room—guests such as J. R. R. Tolkien and others. Enjoying their pipes along with the conversation, the Lewis brothers would often dump their pipe ash on the rug that lay on the floor. The two brothers liked to joke that the ash actually helped to preserve the rug, saying it kept the moths away. It ended up keeping their friends away: Tolkien's wife didn't let him come over to the house after she saw the state it was in after Mrs. Moore had passed away and Maureen had moved out, certain that her husband would get sick if he came around.

The house held even more books when Lewis lived there. Books were stacked from floor to ceiling in most rooms, even along the walls in the hallway and up the staircase. One literary critic described Lewis as the most well-read man in England.

And his house must have looked like it. Lewis liked to joke that his home was held up by books and cobwebs.

Several photos of Lewis hung on the walls of the common room. One was of him in a high-back chair, wearing glasses and a smile. Walter pointed to another one of the pictures and told me that was the last photo ever taken of Lewis. Walter had taken the photo the summer before Lewis passed away. He died the same day the world mourned the death of an all-too-young U.S. president, on November 22, 1963.

I looked over the books on the shelves. They weren't the originals that were there during Lewis's day, but copies of lots of the books he had written. I removed an early edition of *Screwtape Letters* from the shelf and flipped open to the first few pages.

"To J. R. R. Tolkien," the dedication page read.

In addition to old copies of Lewis's books, the bookshelf held some books *about* Lewis—including one or two by Walter. We continued our tour, making our way into a room that had been turned into a library. It had been a garage, but now it held mostly books. Memorabilia from the movie *Shadowlands* was arranged around the room. And the old Eagle & Child sign, which Walter managed to get from the pub and donate to the Kilns, hung from one wall. It was a beautiful, worn metal sign, faded from years in the weather.

Cole led us into the dining room, inviting us to sit at a large table overflowing with tea pots and towering plates of scones and cookies. Several small jars of creams and jellies were sprinkled around the table. The room was filled with the sweet smell of the baked treats.

"This is an official English tea," Rhona told us with a smile as Jen took a seat beside her.

Debbie entered the room at this point in the tour and joined us at the table. After Cole thanked God for the food and the fellowship, she invited us to help ourselves. Debbie taught on C. S. Lewis and J. R. R. Tolkien and literature at a university in Tennessee before taking up the role of warden at the Kilns. Much like Cole, she was born several centuries too late. With grand language and passionate tones, she spoke about her studies in medieval literature and her appreciation for Lewis's and Tolkien's work. She picked up the tour where Walter and Cole had let off, telling us stories about Joy and Lewis and their time together at the home. Her sentences were often prefaced with phrases like, "The thing you have to remember," and "Now keep in mind."

Several photos of Lewis and his wife, Joy, hung on the dining room walls. Lewis had been a bachelor for most of his adult life, not marrying until he was nearly sixty. As we passed around the scones and cookies, filling our plates, Debbie focused the conversation on Joy.

"Joy was a brilliant woman. In fact, she was a prodigy. She graduated from high school in New York at the age of fifteen, and she went on to attend university at that same age."

Debbie told us Joy was also a talented writer (she earned her MA in English Literature from Columbia), and that she was one of the few people—men or women—who was able to keep up with Lewis in a debate.

"The thing you have to remember is she was *very* sharp," Debbie said.

Born to Jewish parents in New York in 1915, Joy was an Atheist and a Communist by the 1930s. But then, to her surprise, God revealed himself to Joy in the 1940s. She had been reading Lewis's writing at the time, whose popularity spread to the States after the publication of his BBC radio broadcast talks during the Second World War. In *The Great Divorce*, *Miracles*, and *The Screwtape Letters*, Joy found a guide for her newfound Christian faith. She and Lewis began to exchange letters back and forth across the Atlantic, which they did for many years before Joy moved to England in the early 1950s, bringing her two young boys (eight and nine years old, respectively) and her fiery, New York attitude with her. Debbie pointed out a photo of Joy holding a rifle hanging on one of the walls in the dining room and told us a story that Joy's son (and C. S. Lewis's stepson), Douglas Gresham, had shared with her.

Apparently Joy had used her gun to scare neighborhood kids off the property after she moved into the house, long after Mrs. Moore had passed away and her daughter, Maureen, had moved out. Not liking the idea of neighborhood kids running around the property, and coming and going as they pleased, Joy would often fire her gun into the air to scare them away.

On one occasion, the three of them, C. S. Lewis, Joy, and Douglas, were walking around the pond behind the house, when they came across a young boy with a bow and arrow. The boy was shooting on the property and, wanting to make sure none of the animals on the property were injured by the boy's arrows, Lewis politely asked him to leave. In response, the boy loaded his bow with an arrow and pointed it at the three of them. Instinctively, Lewis stepped in front of Joy and Douglas, to shield them. That's when he heard Joy's gun cock behind him and her voice cry out, "Get out of my line of fire!"

Everyone in the room laughed as Debbie mimicked Joy's voice and held her arms out like she was holding a rifle.

We took our time that afternoon, eating and talking and laughing in the Kilns dining room, with the view of the garden just beyond the white-framed window. I sat between Jen and Walter, and Steve sat across from us. Cole and Debbie sat at the opposite end of the table, talking with Rhona and her husband. Walter told Jen I was the nicest man he'd ever met, and that he hoped to be as nice as me someday. I laughed, trying not to look as awkward as I felt.

Walter and I talked about Lewis's writing, about the way in which he paired logic and reason with vivid analogies to paint a clear picture of the more complex parts of Christianity.

"That's where his intellect and imagination worked together," Walter said. "It was the perfect combination."

Attempting to invite others into the conversation, Walter told Steve he must hear some great theology from me.

"Ryan's actually quite the writer himself," Steve told Walter.

Walter turned back to me with raised eyebrows. Suddenly, I felt naked all over again. I shrugged, unsure what to say. But when Walter's eyes remained on me, I knew I had to speak up.

"I think there's an opportunity to reach folks in my generation, and the generation coming up behind me. Those who might not otherwise have conversations about theology, but who have questions. *Important* questions." I said. "I'd like to write to them. I'd like to try to help show the beauty and the richness of the Christian narrative. But in a way they'd actually want to read."

"Yes, mmm hmmm," Walter said with a nod.

Still somewhat reluctant to speak openly about my writing, I told Walter about a birthday present Steve had given me a couple summers before we arrived in Oxford: he had some of the writing I had done years before printed and bound as my first, self-published book.

"I'd love to read it," Walter said.

"Yeah? Okay. Well, I'd be honored to share it with you at some point," I told Walter, feeling a bit less naked at this point.

Debbie passed around the plate of scones as we talked. I took a second, which was still warm, and layered on the sweet berry jam. We were still talking when I remembered I had an extra copy of the book Steve had published for me in my bag, which was now sitting beside the front door. A voice from somewhere deep within me met this thought head on: *Wait, what are you doing? You can't actually be considering giving this to him! This is C. S. Lewis's former secretary; what would he possibly think of your writing?!*

After wrestling with this voice for several minutes, I finally excused myself, grabbed the book from my bag, and returned to the table.

"I just remembered I had a spare copy in my bag," I explained, now clutching the well-worn book.

I handed the book across the table to Walter. He looked at its cover, turning it over in his hands, without speaking. Moments felt like ages as I waited for his response.

"I would love to read it," he finally said, lifting his eyes from the book to mine.

I breathed a sigh of relief. The voice in my head stormed off somewhere, slamming the door as it went.

Walter went on to ask me to sign it for him.

We wrapped up our tea in the dining room and Walter led us around the rest of the house. Stopping in the hallway just outside the bathroom, he told us about the time he first met Lewis.

Walter had written back and forth with Lewis for many years before coming to visit for the first time. He was an American teaching English at the University of Kentucky at the time. Some friends who knew Oxford suggested he show up early, as the area wasn't well developed and it was easy to get lost. So he did. Walter's meeting with Lewis was scheduled for a Monday, he showed up at Lewis's front door on Friday.

Walter told us he figured he'd knock on the door, just in case Lewis was home and willing to meet early with him. If not, he'd come back on Monday. So Walter knocked and waited a few moments before the door opened. And there was C. S. Lewis, greeting Walter, and inviting him to come inside.

The two men took their seats in the common room and began catching up, first over one pot of tea, then over a second, and finally, after the third pot of tea, Walter said he grew "increasingly uncomfortable," and had to ask where the bathroom was. Now, as an American who had just arrived in England for the first time, Walter didn't think anything of his own question, but Lewis picked up on Walter's American vocabulary and said, "Of course, I'll show you to the *bathroom*." Lewis led him down the hallway, opened the door of a wardrobe to pull out several towels and a bar of soap, and directed Walter into a small room, closing the door behind him. Walter was left holding these towels and soap in a cramped room that contained only a bathtub and sink.

So there was Walter, in desperate need of a toilet, trying to figure out how he was going to explain this confusion to C. S. Lewis. Finally, after several minutes of drumming up his courage, Walter said he set down the towels and soap and sheepishly wandered back down the hallway to the common room, only to find Lewis seated there, wearing a wide grin. Walter explained that he actually didn't need a bath at all, but what he really needed was a toilet.

"Aha!" Lewis replied. "Well *that* will cure you of those useless American euphemisms! Now, let's begin again. To where would you like to go?"

Note

[1] Matthew Parris, "Why do people debate the future of the church when they have not made up their minds about the existence of God," *The Times,* accessed October 20, 2014, *http://markmeynell.files.wordpress.com/2007/05/matthew-parris-the-heart-of-the-issue.pdf.*

4

Confidence

An Unexpected Book Review

Nearly all my time as an Oxford student was spent in the library. If I wasn't sitting in tutorials or listening to a lecture, I could most likely be found in the library, trying to get through all of my reading before throwing together my weekly essay, hitting "print," and cycling as quickly as I could to my tutorial. Harris Manchester's college library became like a second home to me during my time in Oxford. Early on, I picked out a desk beside a window on the second floor. It had a great view of the jagged Oxford rooftops with chimneys that seemed to stand guard, aimed to poke holes in the blue-grey canopy overhead. And it sat above all the rows of old, musty-scented books on the library's first floor. When it rained, I could watch as the tops of umbrellas bounced and danced along the sidewalks, with shoes shuffling underneath. In the winter, the snow-covered shingled rooftops became a salt and pepper field, the brick chimneys billowing columns of smoke into the sky overhead.

When I wasn't at the Harris Manchester library, I was usually huddled up next to a pile of books on the bottom floor of the Radcliffe Camera, a giant dome of a building, which is part of Oxford University's Bodleian Library. Spanning several buildings, and home to first-edition copies of every book that has ever been printed in England, the Bodleian Library is a treasure trove for anyone with an interest in books. The Bodleian is reserved for members of the university and visiting scholars who gain permission for their research. It is also dead quiet, which made for one particularly embarrassing incident that reminded me how terribly out of place I was.

One day I rushed out of the house to the Bodleian to find a book I needed, without taking the time to silence the worship music playlist on my laptop when I shut it and threw it into my bag. I entered the library and set my things down on an empty seat at an otherwise overflowing table, filled with other students working quietly. I flipped open my laptop to get the call number for the book I needed and my music immediately began blaring.

My heart sank as the voices of Barlow Girl rang out, "I need you to love meee," shattering the silence of the library. Evidently, I had shut the lid of my laptop right in the middle of the chorus, and the girls picked up where they left off, right on cue. I was horrified.

"I'm sorry, I'm sorry. I'm so sorry," I began to whisper, frantically trying to silence my computer, to no avail. Like a bad dream, as much as I pounded away on my keyboard, it would not be muted. The girls continued to sing at the top of their lungs.

"I need you to love meee . . ."

I could feel the weight of all the eyes in the room on me, watching me frantically struggle to quiet my laptop. Finally, a few seconds (which felt like hours) later, I got the idea to shut my laptop, plug in my earphones, and reopen it. It worked. After I had managed to silence the singing, I pulled up the call number for the book I needed and searched for it on the shelves. You can imagine the look on my face when I found the book's spot on the shelf empty. Someone had beaten me to it. My trip to the Bodleian that day had been a complete waste of time. I returned to my seat, packed up my computer, and left, feeling all the eyes in the library trailing me as I went.

I sent Walter a note shortly after our trip to the Kilns, thanking him for showing us around, for sharing his stories of C. S. Lewis, and for taking the time to read my book. I was surprised when he responded right away, inviting Jen and me over for tea.

"Come in, come in," Walter greeted us on a late Sunday afternoon, his voice as warm as the air escaping from his open door.

Photographs lined the walls of Walter's foyer: many of the Pope, and several of Lewis, mostly taken at the Kilns. The last photo ever taken of Lewis was there, the one Walter shot.

He invited us into the living room, where flames danced gently in a fireplace set in the middle of one wall. On either side, bookshelves full of old books with dark, faded spines rose nearly to the ceiling. A tall Greek statue stood in one corner, and an oversized sofa sat in the middle of the room, with a low coffee table before it and two high-back chairs, one on either side of the table.

Walter introduced us to Blessed Lucy of Narnia, his cat, who was perched comfortably on the back of the couch. Enjoying a late-afternoon nap, she didn't notice us.

"Now, I want you to take lots of notes from Jennifer on how to be a lady," Walter told the cat firmly, pointing his finger at her. She lifted her head and blinked slowly at Walter.

Walter showed us into the dining room, where he pointed out a child-sized table in the corner of the room. The table had been built for C. S. Lewis when he was just five years old. He told us Lewis used to work from this table when he was a young boy. Sitting on the table was a tobacco humidor, which Lewis had bought while he was studying at Magdalen College.

Our tour continued, with Walter pointing out several illustrations on another wall. The illustrations were original, framed artwork created for Lewis's book *The Silver Chair*.

Walter invited us to have a seat at the dining table in the middle of the room. Several old books were sitting on it. He'd open the cover of one, introduce it, and then move it in front of us to look at. They were Lewis's old books, from his personal library. Lewis's own handwritten notes filled the margins.

Turning to the back of one of the books, Walter pointed out how Lewis indexed all of his books by subject. He might find something on a particular page that he appreciated, and then he would index it himself in the back of the book for later use. A copy of Dante's work was there, as well as several others. Some of the books were in Latin, some in Italian, and Lewis's notes were in the corresponding language.

Flipping through the pages of these books at Walter's dining room table, and reading Lewis's handwritten notes, I was speechless. I found notes he'd referred to in his autobiography, *Surprised by Joy*, and other books he had written. His handmade appendices made me feel as though I had never properly used a book in my life.

Walter had prepared tea, so we returned to the living room and took our seats in the wingback chairs in front of the fire. He reserved for himself the couch with Blessed Lucy of Narnia resting quietly behind him. She was still curled into a ball, napping on her side.

My book, which I had left with Walter several days before, was resting on the table in front of the fire. Seeing the book sitting there, like an unexpected guest, made my stomach turn and tighten. I had no idea if he had even opened it, let alone what he might think of it when he did.

Walter poured a dollop of milk into our teacups as we sat down and, holding the bowl of sugar, he presented them to us so that we could serve ourselves. Along with the tea, he served "digestive biscuits." Neither Jen nor I had ever tried them before. The name sounded like something you took when you weren't feeling well.

"They'd never get away with calling them that in the States," I told Walter.

"Yes, I know. But they were Lewis's favorite."

"They are semi-sweet," he suggested. Like a graham cracker, but not quite as sweet. They were delicious, especially with the tea, Jen and I both agreed. I had half a dozen before the afternoon was through.

Walter sat on the couch after serving us both, and we began talking about our time in England so far, about C. S. Lewis's writing, and about Walter's own work.

"You know, I'm often asked if I regret having spent all this time studying Lewis's work and compiling his letters. I'm asked if I feel like it's been a waste," Walter confessed to us in his soft-spoken, hybrid American-British accent. "And I don't know how I could. My life is so much *richer* because of this man."

Taking a sharp turn in the conversation, Walter began telling me his thoughts on my book. The knots immediately returned to my stomach.

Walter had been writing for the past forty years. Writing and editing, I should say. Before that, he taught English at the University of Kentucky. From what I could tell, he read prolifically, which is why I was overcome with joy when he shared how he felt about my book.

He told me he thoroughly enjoyed it. He said it was helping him, that he was getting so much from it.

"It is light, but also profound, at the same time," Walter said. "I have never seen someone use Lewis's writings in the way you have. But it didn't make me want to go read Lewis. It made me want to keep on reading *this*.

"You use him as a springboard," Walter said, "rather than simply presenting a regurgitation."

He told me he could not remember the last time he had read a more likable book.

Then he said something I will never forget. And I'm glad Jen was there. Were she not, I would probably still be wondering if that afternoon was actually just a dream.

Walter told me he thought I had written the modern-day *Mere Christianity*. I didn't know whether to laugh or to cry. I told Walter I didn't know what to say, and that his words meant more than he probably realized.

"You must try to get this book published," Walter insisted. "It's not just an experiment; people need to read it."

We left Walter's home that evening feeling warm, even as we stepped out into the cold night air. I laughed out loud, and I gave Jen a look that asked, *Can you believe that?!*

I felt encouraged in a way I could not have imagined before we arrived at Walter's home. I knew at that point that this path had been confirmed for me. Sitting in front of the dancing flames in Walter's living room, I realized, in a way I had not before, that I wanted to write. I wanted to write in a way that might help others see and know the Lord more clearly. The fact that Walter saw something in my writing assured me that I needed to do my best to get it published.

Jen and I spent Thanksgiving in Oxford that year. It was the first time we were away from our families for the holiday. Both of us were thinking about the faces of loved ones around tables, eating plate after plate of turkey and stuffing and pumpkin pie when we made the short walk from our flat in North Oxford to church. Our church's college-aged ministry was hosting a Thanksgiving dinner, even though there was only one other American in the group. But we went, hoping it would dull the pain of being away from our loved ones on the holiday.

I was going through the food line, filling my plate with turkey and fixings, when the guy behind me looked into a bowl of stuffing and asked in a British accent what it was.

"That? That's stuffing," I told him, pointing toward the bowl with a spoon, in a voice someone might have used in response to being asked what a cat was.

"What's in it?" he asked, unfazed by my impatience.

"Well, you know, bread, seasoning . . . it's stuffing," I said, realizing I didn't know exactly what's in stuffing myself, but feeling nevertheless that he should.

Over the next few days, we attended three Thanksgiving dinners, some feeling more American than others, though none of them could compare with being home with our family. That year I learned you can have the greatest spread and the greatest food, but if you're not surrounded by those you love, Thanksgiving is just not the same.

Jen and I were planning on spending our first Christmas in Oxford. We would have liked to spend the holiday with our family, but we didn't have the money for us both to fly home. Steve had enjoyed Oxford so much that he was planning to return to spend the holiday with us in England, knowing it would be difficult to be so far from family for our first Christmas after losing Hayley.

It wasn't long before the holidays arrived that Steve sent me a note telling me he had an idea. Rather than flying to England, he offered to pay for one of our tickets to come home. So at the last minute, we booked two tickets home for Christmas. We shared our plans with no one but Steve, and we arrived at our family's doorstep just a few days before Christmas. They weren't expecting us until the following summer. Jen's mom looked like a cartoon character when she first saw us, her eyes gaping and her jaw on the floor. My grandpa simply stared out from behind his screen door, smiling, before asking, "Are you ghosts?" Many of them cried, as did we.

After months on our own, we treasured the opportunity to be surrounded by those we loved. Jen's parents had been preparing themselves for what would be an unspeakably difficult time, celebrating Christmas with two of their three daughters missing.

"This is the best Christmas present ever," Jen's mom told us with tears in her eyes after the shock finally wore off.

I was happy for a break from the pace of studies. I was thankful for the opportunity to get a proper night's sleep again, and to share our experiences with our community back home. Our friends and family loved hearing about meeting Walter and touring C. S. Lewis's old house. And they encouraged us in some of the more difficult spots of our journey.

"You're not coming back to work for us," my old manager told me over dinner one night in our old hometown. Even though I hadn't actually asked for my old job back, he knew of my struggles with doubt about whether we had made the right decision to go. He made the comment with a smile, only half-joking.

"We won't let you. There are plenty of jobs I could do—I could be a mechanic—but that doesn't mean I'm supposed to."

When Jen's grandfather heard about my plans to try to get my manuscript published, he mentioned that the pastor of their small-town church some twenty years before was now working for one of the country's largest Christian publishers. He gave me his name, and he suggested I try to get in touch with him to see if he could help.

When I first arrived in Oxford, I felt naked even voicing my dreams of writing. And now, just a few months later, C. S. Lewis's former secretary was vouching for my work. I would not have believed it if someone had tried to tell me all of this before it happened. But here I was, writing this publisher from the airport just before boarding my flight back to Oxford. I wrote to introduce myself, to tell him what I hoped to do with my writing, and to see if he might have any words of advice for a first-time author. I would come to find out that this man was not only working for a major Christian book publisher; he was the editor-in-chief. When I first wrote him, I had no idea if I'd actually hear back, or if he'd even read my email. And even if I thought he might, I couldn't have guessed his response.

5

Answered Prayers

A Series of Funny Coincidences

After a month of spending the holidays with friends and family back home, I returned to Oxford on my own. Jen's sister, Leann, and her husband were expecting their first child any day, and Jen didn't want to miss it. As much as I wanted to be there, I could not. School was calling.

Oxford's exam system, like most everything else at the university, is unusual. The only marks that actually count for an Oxford degree are the final exams, which are cumulative, and which come only at the end of the degree. Prior to that, students take what are called collections at the start of each term. Collections are exams that test the student's knowledge of the material they studied the previous term. While they don't actually count for the degree, if students don't do well enough on collections, they are given a few weeks before having to take the collections all over again. Because of Oxford's frantic pace, you really don't want to do that.

After a month of being away, I returned to Oxford to face Greek exams. I spent entire days running through my New Testament notes in the library, until it finally closed late at night. Then I'd hop on my bike and ride to our flat in North Oxford, with my headlight bouncing a beam of light in the dark, where I would study my Greek flash cards until I could no longer keep my eyes open.

Our place felt particularly empty without Jen there. I lived off canned soup and peanut butter sandwiches for weeks, dreaming of the thick-cut steak I had been treated to while home. Knowing my routine, Jen would ask during our calls whether I was making sure to eat dinner. I remember taking a break from Greek flash cards late one Sunday evening to find something to eat, after all the markets had already closed. A lone bottle of ketchup and a box of breakfast cereal was all I found in my fridge and cupboard. Hungry, struggling through Greek, and missing Jen, I wondered all over again what in the world I was doing there.

The ringing noise shook me from my sleep. It was coming from somewhere downstairs. Without moving my head, my arm snaked its way across my body to the nightstand beside my bed, grabbed my alarm clock and brought it within inches of my nearsighted eyes. I blinked to see the time: 3:05. Only an hour and a half after I had gone to bed. My body shuddered.

The ringing noise downstairs continued, so I forced my tired body out of bed and dragged it to the base of the stairs where my laptop sat, illuminating the carpeted steps. Jen had told me the night before that they thought this might be the night her sister and brother-in-law would welcome their daughter into the world. She told me I ought to leave my laptop on so that she could Skype with me, just in case.

All of this was a fuzzy memory as I sat on the bottom step and pulled the computer onto my lap, my eyes straining to see the monitor clearly. I pressed the phone icon, accepting Jen's Skype call.

"Hey!" Jen said in an alarmingly chipper voice, wearing an ear-to-ear smile and holding a swaddled baby in her arms. "Look who I have!"

Something I have envied in Jen since we first met is that she has always known exactly what she wants to be: she wants to be a mother. And, from the very early on, I knew she'd make an incredible one. In fact, that's one of the reasons I asked for her hand in marriage.

I wanted children, too, but I also wanted to be in a good spot, financially. There were things I wanted in place. I guess I'd say I wanted to be responsible about it. And that meant putting the brakes on having our own children, much to Jen's heartbreak. While she was encouraging me to apply to Oxford, while she was leaving her job and setting out with me on this journey, she knew full well she was putting her dreams of having children of our own on hold.

"Say hi to your new niece, Khloe," Jen told me, propping the baby's face closer to the computer screen. Tears and laughter came over me with a rush.

"Hey, baby Khloe," I said, now more awake.

We spoke for a while in the quiet, early morning hours of that day. I congratulated my in-laws, and I laughed with Jen and her parents at the faces Khloe made. Afterward, as I crawled back under my blankets for a couple more hours of sleep, I wondered if everyone would forgive me for missing this moment. I wondered if I would forgive myself. And, even more, I wondered how I would feel about it at the end of our journey, if ever there was such a thing.

Jen returned to Oxford several weeks after I did. I passed my collections—just barely in Greek—and had settled into my new tutorials. Being reunited with Jen made life feel complete again. After a week of allowing herself to readjust to the time difference, Jen was determined to begin her job search. Money was tight, and we knew we would need to find something that would provide a bit of income if we were going to make it. We also knew it would be good for Jen to have something to fill her time.

I was in the library the Monday Jen was planning to start looking for work. It was not yet noon when my phone began ringing, interrupting the library's silence. I was surprised that it wasn't Jen calling, but I hurled myself down the stairs and out the double doors, into the empty corridor to take the call, hoping to avoid disturbing the other students all over again.

"Hello, this is Ryan," I said, gasping after my near sprint out of the library.

"Hi, Ryan, this is Debbie Higgens, warden at the Kilns. How are you?"

It had been several months since Debbie had prepared tea for us at the Kilns with Cole, Walter, Rhona, and her husband, so it took me a minute to remember her. Once I had, I wondered why she might be calling.

"Sorry to bother you, Ryan, but I'm calling because I have a question for you."

Debbie explained to me that, with Cole preparing for exams, and her attending to her other duties at the house, she needed some extra help leading tours of the Kilns.

"I know you're busy with school, but I was wondering if that was something you would mind helping with?"

The line sat dead for a few seconds as I waited for a catch. I waited for Debbie to say that, in exchange, she'd need my first unborn child or something. But she didn't.

"Hello . . . Ryan?"

"Yes, hi. Sorry, Debbie," I said, shaking myself from my shocked stupor. "Yes, of course. I'd love to help."

"Great! That's wonderful news. Perhaps you can come by this Saturday and join me for a tour? That way you can get some practice with me, and then we can talk about when you might be able to start."

"Yeah, that'd be great."

"Oh, and one more thing. Is there any chance Jen might be looking for some extra work? If so, I could use a bit of help with paperwork and a few other things around here."

I laughed out loud, explaining to Debbie the curious timing of her call, and how Jen was planning to begin her job search that day. I also told her Jen had no idea where she was going to start looking.

"Well I had been praying about this, Ryan, and your names came to me, so I thought I'd give you a call. I'm glad I did!"

———————————— ❧ ————————————

I received an email from Dr. Michael Ward a few weeks into winter ("Michaelmas") term. Dr. Ward is a C. S. Lewis expert in Oxford. He wrote his doctoral dissertation on his theory that the common, symbolic thread that unites the books in the *Chronicles of Narnia* series is, of all things, medieval cosmology. His dissertation received quite a bit of attention when it was published. The BBC ran a documentary about it, and the New Testament scholar N. T. Wright referred to Dr. Ward as the foremost living Lewis scholar.

As a past president of the C. S. Lewis Society, Dr. Ward acted as an advisor for the group. I first met him at a dinner before one of the Society meetings the term before I received this email. Outside of that meeting, we hadn't talked. *What could he possibly want to meet with me for?* I wondered.

We met at Dr. Ward's offices in St. Peter's house, a nearly empty room on the second floor that overlooked the college quad, and then stepped out for a short walk to a French restaurant just around the corner, the winter air revealing our breath. He wore a stocking cap to cover his otherwise bare head.

Dr. Ward spoke in what was perhaps the most posh, articulate English accent I had heard. I had never seen him without a suit and tie, and he was as bright as anyone I had met in this city, all of which made me feel rather intimidated. Thankfully, his dry sense of humor helped to ease my nerves.

We were seated at a table beside a window that looked out at foot traffic along George Street. The restaurant staff was dressed in white and black, and the smell of roasted root vegetables and red meat floated through the air.

After asking about my decision to come to Oxford, and hearing about how my journey had been shaped by C. S. Lewis's work, Dr. Ward asked if I knew that the current C. S. Lewis Society president was set to graduate that spring.

"Yeah, I heard that."

"Well, is there any chance you might be interested in taking up the role next year?"

Trying to hide my shock, I told Dr. Ward I couldn't imagine anything else at Oxford to which I'd rather give my time.

"Excellent," he said, his eyes beaming behind his gold-framed glasses.

He told me the Society members would have to vote on the decision, of course, but that he would personally recommend me for the role.

"Oh, and there's just one other thing," he continued. "From now on, please call me Spud. All my friends do."

Spud? I thought to myself. It seemed like such a funny request. Too informal.

"Yes, of course," I assured him. But before the end of the night, I was already failing to keep my promise. He really didn't look like a "Spud."

About a month after returning to Oxford, I received a note from the publisher I had emailed before leaving the States, apologizing for the delay in getting back to me.

Hi Ryan,

I am sorry that it took so long for this email to reach me. Since it was not sent directly to my email address, it took some time for it to work its way through our system to get to me. I received it this morning.

Indeed, I was pastor of Nooksack Valley Baptist Church in Everson, Washington, from 1963–68! What

a surprise to receive an email from the husband of
one of Daryl and Dorothy's granddaughters. It hardly
seems possible, but it has been nearly forty-three years
since we left Everson, so it does make sense.

Yes, I would like to see a copy of your manuscript.
Send it to my email address as an attachment.

Taken aback by his willingness to help, I replied immediately,
attaching my manuscript. I wondered what he might think, and
I cringed, knowing I would have to wait to find out.

I had never been a tour guide before working at the Kilns, but
it felt surprisingly natural. Tour guests ranged from Americans
who were thrilled to be in the home where Lewis once lived and
wrote; to Korean exchange students from London who spoke
little English; to uninterested kids who had been dragged along
by their parents; to elderly British women visiting with a group
from their local parish.

Sometimes guests would listen with eyes the size of half-dollars, laughing at all my jokes and getting teary-eyed at the more
emotional stories. Other times, guests would fall asleep in their
chairs, tired from overnight flights, only to wake with a jolt and
look around the room to see if anyone had noticed.

I began my tours by asking the guests to introduce themselves and tell me a little about what had brought them to the
Kilns. I'd ask about their knowledge of Lewis's life and works,
trying to find the resident Lewis expert so I could turn to them
in the event I was stumped. They'd usually get red in the face
when I'd tell them to be ready for any questions I couldn't answer.

My favorite guests were the ones who had only a faint knowledge of Lewis. The ones who maybe knew something about the *Chronicles of Narnia* series, but not much else. I loved to tell them about this man who spent hours each day replying to all of the letters he received, never using a typewriter, but always a dip pen. Lewis believed writers should think about the cadence of their written words, and he believed the clickety-clack of the typewriter keys got in the way. He also believed having to stop and dip his pen every so often helped his creativity.

I told them the story of Walter and the "bathroom." I'd share that Lewis was fond of going for swims in the pond behind his house, and how I struggled to picture it, mostly because I always pictured Lewis wearing a tweed jacket and smoking a pipe. I would ask them to imagine Lewis's house filled with books—stacked not only on bookshelves, but lining the hallways and even in piles stacked up the spiral staircase. And I loved telling them about this man whose friend had to interfere in his finances, creating two accounts for Lewis's money: one that he had access to, and one that would be used to help those who were in a pinch and wrote asking for help. These arrangements were made not so that Lewis would be more giving, but so that he wouldn't give away all his money. At this point in the tour, I'd usually share one of my favorite Lewis quotes, from *Mere Christianity*: "If our charities do not at all pinch or hamper us, I should say they are too small. There ought to be things we should like to do and cannot do because our charitable expenditure excludes them."

———————————— ✧ ————————————

One of my favorite parts about the Kilns was actually not at the house, but just beyond it. The Kilns sat at the foot of Shotover Hill, which was a nature reserve. Between the Kilns and the ascent of Shotover Hill was a small pond, surrounded by tall trees, and beside the pond was a small brick bench where C. S. Lewis used to sit, smoke his pipe, and reflect. It was a quiet, peaceful spot. Every so often I would arrive early to the Kilns and I would take a seat on the bench to watch the ducks float by on the pond's mirrored surface.

I was seated there on this bench one sunny morning when I realized what an oasis this area was amid the otherwise frantic pace of life in Oxford. The sound of wild birds singing was the only noise I heard that morning. I imagined Lewis rowing his punt across the water, removed from the demands of life as an Oxford don, free from the teaching and speaking engagements. Escaping, for a moment, the duty of responding to the thousands of letters he received from fans around the world.

Lewis had it figured out, I thought to myself. When I stood to make my way down the hill toward the Kilns for the morning's tour, I noticed for the first time the blue-and-white speckled sky reflected on the water's surface. As I walked along the water's edge, a leaf fell from one of the trees just in front of me, floating gently on the air before landing on the water's surface, dashing the reflection of the sky into shards.

This falling leaf had shattered the sky's reflection on the water's surface, but the sky itself had not changed, of course. The sky was still there, just as it had always been. And somehow, in that moment, this picture reminded me of the time when I was fourteen and my mom returned home one evening with tears in her eyes. I cannot now remember what it was, but something terrible had unfolded in her life and she told me she no longer believed in God. This woman who I knew as one of the bubbliest persons in my life told me she was certain that, if God really did exist, he would not have allowed whatever had happened to happen. She told me she was done with church.

I was an adult when my mom told me about growing up in the Jehovah's Witness Church. My grandpa and grandma raised her and her siblings in the Jehovah's Witness tradition until my uncle's high school girlfriend became pregnant and they were no longer welcomed by the Jehovah's Witnesses. That's when my grandparents turned their back on the church. Not just on Jehovah's Witnesses, but religion of any kind. As did my mom, for many years.

As a young boy, I grew up in and out of church (though never attending with the Jehovah's Witnesses). We would visit a nearby Protestant church on Sunday mornings, and we'd usually go for a few weeks. But then, inevitably, something would be wrong with the church, and we'd stop going, only to join a new church a while later.

Sometimes I think the fact that I'm a Christian today is a not-so-small miracle.

That afternoon my mom told me, with tears in her eyes, that she was done with church and God, I cried, too. I was sad, and angry. But mostly, I was disappointed. I remember telling her she couldn't *not* believe in God. I told her it didn't make sense to believe in God only when things go as we'd like. Sometimes really, really bad things happen to us, I told her, and sometimes they happen to others. And I tried to explain, using whatever words a fourteen-year-old might use to explain such a thing, that God either does or does not exist, whether life goes the way we think it ought to or not.

But she did not budge. She held her ground. And I knew I had a decision to make.

I decided I really did believe in God, even when my mom decided she could not. I began attending church on my own, finding rides with whoever was able to take me until I turned sixteen and could finally drive myself. It would take many years for my mom to trust God again.

Walking beside the pond and watching the sky's reflection shatter into fragments of blues and whites, knowing the sky overhead was left untouched, reminded me of this conversation with my mom. It reminded me that the reality of God is not broken by the brokenness of our world. Creation, we're told, is deathly sick. Stumbling about on broken legs. But it is not abandoned. God does not always give us answers for our questions about the nightmares of this life, but from time to time he does offer gentle reminders of his presence—even if only a leaf falling on a pond.

⁂

Jen and I stayed in on the last Friday of Michaelmas term, after I handed in my final essay. We enjoyed a rare slow-paced dinner together, and then we played a board game some friends gave us as a going-away present. I loved that time, just the two of us, sharing laughs.

About halfway through the second game of the night, my thoughts drifted to our new lives in England. About leaving home, and all of the changes we had experienced over the past six months.

"This is kind of a weird thought," I said to Jen as she stared down at the cards in her hand, "but what do you think our parents would have thought if someone had told them, when we were still young kids running around, that the two of us would one day become best friends, get married, and move to Oxford? That we'd be sitting here twenty-some years later playing a board game together in England?"

Jen looked up from her cards, across the table at me. "Yeah, that is a weird thought," she said. "Now play."

I smiled. That's my wife: tough as nails.

———— ⟨⟩ ————

I was at the Kilns one sun-drenched Saturday afternoon when I heard back from the editor-in-chief of the Christian publishing company I had been in touch with.

> Ryan,
>
> I do not have the time to read the whole manuscript, but after reading about fifty pages I decided it was something I should pass on to one of our editors for consideration. (I should also mention that I took it home, and my wife read parts of it as well, and she liked your writing style and thought it had possibilities.)
>
> So I forwarded the attached document to our editor with the recommendation that she give it a careful look. I have been in publishing for over thirty years, and one thing I have learned is that top-down publishing decisions seldom lead to successful publications. If the people who have the primary responsibility for acquiring, editing, marketing, and selling books are not sold on a book's potential, it is fruitless for the person at the top of the ladder to impose a

decision on the group. Most of all, every book needs an editor who will be the evangelist or champion for the book. And that editor has to be so enthusiastic about the book that they can "sell" it to the rest of the publishing team responsible for the book. So that is where the process is now.

In the amount of time it took me to read this note, I received another email, this time from the acquisitions editor he had mentioned. Jen had entered the room at this point. She began reading over my shoulder.

Hi Ryan,

I am sorry that I have not yet let you know that I am reviewing your project! I took a quick look and enjoyed what I read. Unfortunately, I have been quite busy and traveling over the last couple of weeks, but I look forward to getting into the manuscript and giving it a more careful read. I certainly appreciate your premise and all that you have to bring to the topic. I must also add that I noticed that you lived in Bellingham for a time. I went to college at WWU in Bellingham and still miss the lovely town.

So—yes, I will read more carefully and discuss your proposal with our acquisitions committee. Thank you for giving us the opportunity to review and consider it.

Seated there in the Kilns, beaming at the two emails, I could hardly believe it. I was over the moon, as they say. Of course, this would only make the looming fall hurt that much more.

6

Wilderness

When It Rains It Pours Here, Too

Most Oxford colleges host formal dinners for their students and faculty every week. It's one of many Oxford traditions. These dinners are a time to get dressed up, to enjoy a break from studies, and to share a laugh. As busy as things were, I forced myself to attend at least a couple of the formal college dinners each term. They were good for me, I told myself. I needed the break. I also thought it would be a good idea to actually have a conversation with other members of the college, something I wasn't always good at making time for.

Formal dinners are about like any other social event, with small talk and predictable questions. "So, what are you studying?" "What do you plan on doing with your degree?" Questions that make my skin bristle, but which I tell myself are good for me. Not so unlike a parent telling their children to eat their vegetables.

While I was reluctant to talk about my writing aspirations when I first arrived in Oxford, as the year progressed, I found myself more and more willing to confess these dreams. I began to share, quite openly, my intentions for using my theology studies to write about the Christian faith in a way that people who wouldn't normally be interested in theology might actually enjoy. This came across like a bad joke.

After a faint smile, and thinly veiled amusement, the dinner guest next to me would often say something like, "Writing? Is there any money in that?"

"How about you?" I'd ask, turning the attention away from myself. "What are your plans after graduation?"

"Well, I am in talks with such and such country about being an ambassador," they'd say, in full seriousness. And I'd nod a knowing nod, take a sip of wine, and feel suddenly very tiny sitting there in my chair, dressed in a suit and bowtie. Checking my watch and gazing at the large portraits that hung on the walls around the room, I'd feel as though I had shown up to the wrong party.

At times, I felt like I was sitting in a room surrounded not by people, but by caricatures. A young man with dark, slicked-back hair, with a tux and a strong chin—an athlete, I believe—guzzling wine from his shiny black shoe to a great round of applause. A beautiful blonde girl in a black gown, smiling and pretending to be amused by the table conversation, in case our fellow student really did wind up becoming the ambassador to such and such country after all. Perhaps we are all caricatures of ourselves, at times, playing the roles we're expected to play. Of course, it is awfully easy to play the caricature when you're bound in a suit and bowtie or cinched in a gown. But when the whole world is making small talk, an honest conversation with a real human being can make you feel like a person again.

Formal dinners were not all bad. The food was always delicious, and there was so much of it, at six courses. One evening, I found myself sitting next to a girl with tightly curled, dark-brown hair and a broad smile. Her name was Rosie, and she might be one of the kindest people I've ever met. This usually makes me suspicious. You know what I mean, when someone is so nice you can't help but wonder if they're really just as mean as the rest of us when you're not around.

After some small talk, I asked Rosie if she really was as kind as she seemed.

"I don't know," she told me, pausing to think. "I was riding my bike the other day when a man stepped out into the street and I nearly hit him! I thought some not-so-nice things about him."

That's when I figured Rosie might actually be as nice as she seemed. I went on to ask about her dreams. She told me she was fond of sewing and making clothes.

"I made this," she told me, pointing proudly to her dress.

After another moment of thinking about my question, she spoke up again.

"I want to make beautiful things."

And with that simple, honest sentence, Rosie put into words something I had not previously been able to. In that moment, I realized that I, too, wanted to make beautiful things.

Even in the awkwardness of formal dinners and being made to feel as small as the conversation, I became more and more certain that writing about theology in a beautiful way was what I was being called to do. Whether I was being heckled by a soon-to-be diplomat or not.

Jen and I spent our first spring abroad traveling around Europe with her parents and some close friends of our family. I had nearly two months off from school, so we spent time seeing more of England, flying to Rome, and then continuing on to Paris.

We watched young sheep play tag behind stone fences on the rolling hills in the English countryside. We passed by two girls in their matching school uniforms sitting on a wood footbridge, dangling their feet over the edge as they watched a stream meander beneath them in an old watermill village. We stood in front of Stonehenge for a photo, me hugging my ears with my shoulders.

We saw the Pope address a crowd in Rome. We walked through his museum with our jaws on the floor, and we stared in awe at Michelangelo's *Pietà*, which nearly brought me to tears. We ate pizza at a table tucked away in an old Italian alley, with clothes hanging on lines that spanned the buildings overhead. And we strolled along the hills of the city's ancient ruins, gazing skyward at trees that shot bare and high into the air before exploding into a canopy of leaves, looking like something out of a Dr. Seuss book. In Paris, I was taken aback by just how small the *Mona Lisa* is. We watched the sun go down behind the city's horizon from atop the Eiffel Tower before taking a late-night boat ride along the River Seine, with moonlight on the water's surface guiding our way.

On our last day in Paris, I received an unexpected note: an email from the acquisitions editor at the Christian publisher.

Dear Ryan,
Thanks so much for giving us the opportunity to read your manuscript. I read it and had our

acquisitions team and another editor take a look at it also. We all enjoyed your warm and conversational writing style and your skill with presenting some big concepts and ideas in a very approachable and interesting way. You have some real skill with language and presentation and I think there would be openness to your voice.

Unfortunately, after much conversation and some discussion with folks who make decisions in the sales and marketing departments, we don't feel that we can move forward with the project. The marketplace is so competitive these days and without a following it's hard to sell a book unless it is obviously on a topic people want to know about. I would like to leave the door open for you to contact me at any time, though.

I'm so sorry to have to decline your proposal but please do feel free to send me other ideas or stay in touch as other things grow and change for you. I'm delighted to think of you at the Kilns.

I walked the short trip from our hotel to the Eiffel Tower, found a seat on a bench in the park, and began to pray. I told God I suddenly felt very unsure about the calling in which I had previously been confident. *Had I misheard you?* I asked God silently, with tears in my eyes. *Is this not what you would have for me?*

I wondered why we would come this far only to face rejection. I told God that if this was something he genuinely wanted me to pursue, that I'd need him to assure me of it. Even though I did not know what that kind of assurance would even look like.

After nearly twenty minutes of this one-sided conversation, I began walking back to our hotel, following the same path I took to get there. I hadn't made it thirty feet before a paper gospel tract, written completely in French, caught my eye. The tract showed two pencil-drawn characters talking, with one introducing the other to the story of Jesus, who had sunbursts radiating from somewhere just behind his head. Sitting there so peacefully in the soil beside a small shrub, the tract stopped me mid step. Wiping the tears from my eyes, I bent down to pick it up, wondering how I had not seen it before.

Spring term started like a shot. After returning to Oxford from our European travels, I took two, three-hour handwritten collections in one day. By the end, my head was spinning and I couldn't feel my thumb and forefinger. Jen spent that same day in London, at the royal wedding, with a group of her girlfriends. They took their spot in front of Westminster Abbey at three o'clock in the morning and managed to be just five people back when the Queen, the Prince, Kate, and others made their way into the historic church. Yet, even with my numb thumb and crippled hand, I was pretty sure I came out on top of that deal.

Beyond returning to collections and a whole new course load, spring term—or Trinity Term, as it's called—came with new challenges. When it came time to pay for the rest of the year's tuition and fees, I realized that not only were we going to be unable to pay for the following year's studies, but that we were actually short for the last term of my first year.

I shared this with Jen. She was just as unsure as I was what this would mean for us. She was now working as much as possible at the Kilns, helping Debbie with cleaning, scheduling tours, and anything else that she could. I was giving as many tours as I could make time for. But it was clear that, short of a miracle, we would not be returning for my second year of studies. Night after night, I would lie in bed, staring up at the ceiling with tears warming my cheeks. And when I knew Jen had fallen asleep, I'd let the tears fall more freely. I wondered what in the world I had done. Without any spoken words, I'd ask God if I had somehow misunderstood. *What does this mean for my calling?* I would ask.

When it rains here in Oxford, as elsewhere, it pours.

On May first, Jen and I floated through Oxford with roses in hand on a punt along the River Cherwell. It was the one-year anniversary of saying good-bye to Jen's sister Hayley, a scene neither one of us could have imagined before her death. Death was always something we read or heard about other families going through, not ours. But it had happened, and the six thousand miles that now separated us from our family made this loss even more difficult.

I had never been on a punt before. Fortunately Jen had, so she took the responsibility of steering us down the slow-moving river, past cattle grazing on the grassy shore. She held the long pole in her hands, pushing off the muddy river bottom, using the pole like a rudder to steer the narrow boat north along the water.

While Jen steered, and the boat rocked gently from side to side, I sat in the middle of the punt, removing the plastic wrapping from the pink roses we had picked up from Sainsbury's.

Then, one at a time, Jen and I began sharing our favorite memories of Hayley.

Standing in the back of the boat, with her hands gripped to the metal pole and her eyes glued to the water in front of us, Jen shared her memories of watching Hayley as a cheerleader. She remembered her smile, how happy she seemed. She remembered watching Hayley being tossed high into the air, and then coming back down, safely, still wearing that contagious grin.

When I could tell Jen was finished, I placed a pink rose on the river. We watched as it floated slowly on the water's surface behind us.

I shared my memory of the time Hayley insisted that she could lift me, and then actually carried me in her arms across the room. I laughed with tears in my eyes at the memory, and in that moment, I could still hear Hayley's laughter. When the smile had faded from my face and Hayley's laugh had faded from my ears, I placed another rose on the water, and we continued north along the river.

Jen shared about how Hayley helped her coach middle school volleyball. She recounted how great Hayley was with those young girls. The longing was visible in Jen's face, the "what if?" that comes when someone passes at such a young age. I placed a rose on the water, and then I told about the time I flew across Washington State at the last minute to see Hayley cheer at the state basketball tournament her senior year. I recounted the look on her face when she didn't believe I had actually flown in to make it in time. Rose on the water. Jen shared about her memories of Hayley dressed up in her pink prom dress, and how everyone said she looked like she had just stepped out of a fairy tale. Another rose on the water. I shared about the time Hayley told me, when I had been dragging my feet on having children, that Jen and I had to have our first child before she left for college. Before she was gone. More roses on the water.

Soon there was a string of roses on the water. A silent parade of roses and tears and memories of our sister, all following us as we glided along the mirror surface of the Cherwell River.

It was there, on that punt in Oxford, that I realized memories are one of God's most under-rated gifts.

Jen and I attended St. Andrew's Church when we first arrived in Oxford, a smallish Anglican church just down the lane from our flat in North Oxford. Around Christmastime, we began attending St. Aldate's, a larger, charismatic, evangelical Anglican church with lots of graduate students, in the heart of Oxford's city center. Many of our friends from school attended St. Aldate's, and I quickly fell in love with the teaching of a vicar by the name of Simon.

Simon was the most American Brit I had met. His preaching wardrobe changed very little from week to week, consisting almost solely of knee-length cargo shorts, a leather waistcoat, and a plaid button-up shirt, with slip-on shoes. Thick and wide-shouldered with a booming voice to match, Simon leaned with his full weight on the podium when he preached, staring out at the crowded church. He frequently mentioned his former career as a butcher, which explained why his teaching was so meat-and-potatoes. He had little time for pretense. I appreciated that most about him.

Simon gave a message one Sunday evening in St. Aldate's that will forever stand out in my mind. Taking his spot behind the lectern, and leaning heavily on it as he always did, Simon spoke candidly to all of us there.

"As you know, we're going through a series on Romans," Simon began. "I spent more than twenty hours this week preparing a message on Romans." He paused, thinking about his words carefully. "But then, during the prayer this evening, there was a line and I thought there might be something else I ought to speak on tonight. How's that for being a charismatic?"

Laughter trickled through the crowded room.

Simon went on to share the story of Jesus being led into the wilderness immediately after his baptism, and he pointed out that what is so often missed in this story is that the Bible says Jesus was led into the wilderness by the Holy Spirit. This was not a minor point, Simon insisted. He talked about how this time in the wilderness was intentional, not a chance wandering, and how it prepared Jesus for the mission the Father had for him. Simon went on to speak about his own challenging experiences in the wilderness, as well as the challenges others have faced in their own pursuit of God's call on their lives.

He told a story about a well-known preacher who had found great fame for his speaking gifts and who, at one point in his ministry, was bed-ridden by a sudden onset of Tourette syndrome. This man who was so well known for his silky smooth speech could not even leave his bedroom for fear of the crass language that spewed like venom from his tongue.

Simon then shared about a word this same man later received from God. After weeks of lying in his bed, wondering why he would be so accursed, he heard God tell him, "This is who you would be without me. Your gifts are to be used for my glory, not for yours."

Without this traumatic experience, Simon explained, the preacher would not have been able to pursue God's calling on his life because he would have believed that all of the praise he received was about him, not God.

"I wasn't expecting to give this talk tonight," Simon concluded. "But I hope this word comes as an encouragement to any who might be in the wilderness."

Simon told us he did not know why God had stopped him at the last minute from giving the message he had spent so many hours preparing, but that maybe there was someone in the room who needed to know that even *this* challenge would be used for God's glory, and to prepare them for the call on their life.

I wrote Simon shortly after he gave that impromptu message about the wilderness, to introduce myself, and to tell him that his message could not have come at a more perfect time. I asked if he might be willing to meet to talk in person.

We met on Pembroke Street, just across from Christ Church. Simon was wearing long cargo shorts, a brown-leather waistcoat, and slip-on shoes, and I realized then this was not just his preaching wardrobe.

"How about some ice cream?" Simon asked, shaking my hand in a firm grip.

I double-checked my watch. Indeed, it was ten in the morning.

"Sure, yeah," I said, trying to hide my surprise. "Sounds great."

My tongue found chunks of frozen strawberries in the sweet ice cream as we crossed the street and made our way to Christ Church meadow, a riverside park beyond the college's high stone walls. Punts were floating the river, students were lying on the lawns reading, and large cattle grazed in the neighboring fields.

"You know, I'm the most American Brit you'll meet," Simon told me, making our way toward the river's edge.

"Oh, yeah?"

"Yeah. Well, at least, that's what I'm told."

"I could see that," I told him. "You wear your heart on your sleeve, like we Americans. You tell it like it is. I appreciate that."

"I do, yeah," he said in agreement. "I used to be a butcher, you know. And a meat salesman. So I'm pretty to the point. 'You want this cut, it costs this much.'"

We passed several people on our walk, most of whom Simon seemed to know, and who knew him. Lots of smiles and hellos. Eventually, we sat on a bench that overlooks the river and watched the water pass by.

"So you wrote me wanting to talk about something," Simon said, taking the final bite of his ice cream cone, without removing his gaze from the river.

"Yeah, it was about your sermon. The one where you talked about how sometimes God leads us into the wilderness. And how God uses these seasons to form us into who he wants us to be, to be prepared in a way we wouldn't be otherwise."

"Ah, yes," he said, still looking off somewhere into the river.

"That message really shook me up," I told him.

I shared with Simon about how we had left home for Oxford to pursue what we believed to be God's call. I confessed that even though this was a dream come true, in many ways it was also one of the most difficult things Jen and I had ever done. I went on to tell Simon about Hayley's unexpected death, just months before we left home, and how that had made this experience that much more difficult for the both of us, but especially for Jen.

"This has been particularly tough on my wife," I said. "Adjusting to life in a foreign country has been pretty lonely for her. But the grief of losing her sister . . ."

Simon hung his head, shaking it back and forth as though he felt the weight of this loss.

"How is she doing with all of this," he asked.

"It hasn't been easy on her, by any means. But she's tough. Tougher than I am. And supportive, even when she's struggling. There's no way I could have done this without her."

Simon asked what I wanted to do after Oxford, a question I had been asked many times since arriving.

"When I first came over, I figured I'd go the PhD route and study to eventually become a professor," I told him. "I knew I wanted to write and speak, so I figured the degree would let me do that on the side.

"But since coming here," I continued, "I've begun to think maybe that's not where I'm supposed to be. I really enjoyed speaking and writing in my former job, so I know I'd love to do that. But I think I'd like to do that on questions about faith and God and life, for a general audience. Not just for academics. To help everyday people see him more clearly."

I paused, to think about what I said, my eyes glued to the river.

"I know it sounds like a pipe dream, but if I could do that, if I could write and speak to help others with their faith, that's what I'd be doing."

"We need both of those things, Ryan, writing and speaking," Simon said. "And there are a lot of people who don't want to do those things. I enjoy speaking, but writing is a chore. If you can do both of those things, then I don't think that's a pipe dream."

I nodded, still chewing on his words. We left our spot beside the river and walked back toward the gate through which we had entered the meadow. As we approached the entrance, Simon spoke up again.

"God has a call on your life, and it is being equipped here," he said, looking me straight in the eyes. "And whilst there will be some joy and delight in pursuing that, experience shows it will be contested at various levels. You are devoting your life to defending and contending for the gospel. That's front line; you can expect incoming fire, spiritually, emotionally, relationally, practically . . ."

Simon paused, giving his words room to breathe.

"You know, Ryan, you have to gain this knowledge, you have to get this degree, to do what you want to do. And this is a great place to get it." His eyes left me to roam Christ Church and the meadow before returning to mine. "But I think you'll realize, afterward, that God brought you here for more than just a degree. He's teaching you both through all of this, and you might not know how until much later."

7

Regret

Saying Good-Bye to Oxford

xford is a city of ideas, filled with people passionate about
ideas. On any given night, you can listen to world-leading
thinkers in nearly any subject imaginable: theoretical physics,
cognitive psychology, or international politics. Prime minis-
ters visit to give talks, as do Hollywood film stars. My first year
in Oxford saw the famous atheist Richard Dawkins making
an appearance onstage, as well as, perhaps a bit surprisingly,
Pamela Anderson. On nights when I could leave my studies long
enough to hear a lecture, I had a hard time choosing which to
attend and which I could live with missing.

The one lecture I was almost always sure to catch was at
the weekly Oxford University C. S. Lewis Society meeting.
The second-story room of Pusey House where the Society met
was adorned with green wallpaper with gold accents. Its stone
window frames looked out at St. John's castle-like college. Pusey
House was just down the street from The Eagle & Child pub, no

coincidence I am sure. Sometimes the meeting would involve a professor presenting a paper that she had prepared for an academic journal. On other evenings, the talk would be more personal, with a slide show and someone sharing his memories of C. S. Lewis the tutor, say, or godfather, or stepfather, even. The Society was filled with wonderful, tweed-jacketed folks, several of whom had long beards. It was not unusual for members to quote Lewis, G. K. Chesterton, or George MacDonald at great length in conversation, with eyes closed and a sweeping, dreamy smile, or tears in their eyes.

The meetings were also frequented by fresh-faced Americans, young and old fans of C. S. Lewis who were in the city for a semester abroad, or on vacation, looking polished and out of place. But it was the sweet, quirky, long-standing members whom I so loved and whom I hoped not to let down when I became society president my first spring in Oxford. I did my best not to let my own naïveté and seemingly inadequate knowledge of the Inklings, outside of Lewis, make the wheels come off of this long-standing Oxford University society. And perhaps I tried too hard. Perhaps that's why I so often found myself with my foot in my mouth.

At the end of my first evening as president, I stood in front of the room to ask everyone there to join me in thanking the evening's speaker, only to find myself asking everyone to thank *me* for coming. A roar of laughter filled the room, followed by a round of applause, and one very red face. After the laughter quieted down, I corrected myself and secretly hoped that no one would cast a vote to confirm I was not fit to be president and hurl me out the second-story window. This was actually a reoccurring fear of mine during my tenure. I took comfort in thinking that surely if enough people decided the second-story window was the best solution for me, my dear friend Walter would speak up in his soft, patient voice and ask the mob to reconsider.

I shared the publisher's rejection letter with Walter that spring, though not without hesitation. I felt like I had let Walter down, and I was worried he would feel the same. But rather than scorn me, Walter told me about how even Tolkien's *Lord of the Rings* was not accepted when he first pitched it to publishers. He went on to remind me that C. S. Lewis struggled for years to get his writing published to a wide audience. Walter told me that, from a young age, Lewis dreamt of being a poet, and that even after a couple early books of poetry, Lewis never received widespread acclaim for his early work. In fact, C. S. Lewis didn't become well known as a writer until he was in his thirties, after his conversion to Christianity. It was only after he wrote an imaginary correspondence between an elder demon and his young apprentice that Lewis became widely known as a writer.

Oh, you'll be a writer, God could perhaps be seen saying in Lewis's life. *But not in a way you could have ever imagined.*

"Do not give up," Walter insisted.

After talking it over with an author friend back in the States— who insisted that this publisher taking the time to get back to me, and not simply sending a generic response, was confirmation of my writing—I took his advice and introduced myself to a handful of literary agencies. As I was told, most publishers these days are hesitant to even talk with a first-time author directly. I did some research into the kinds of things literary agencies typically like to see from prospective authors and I began putting together my pitch, while doing my best to keep up with my studies. I was beginning the research for my graduating thesis at this point— which I was writing under Dr. Michael Ward's supervision, who still insisted on my calling him "Spud"—preparing to wrap up my first year at Oxford.

As it turns out, securing a literary agent is no easy task. Literary agents aren't likely to take on any projects they don't think will actually be picked up by a publisher. Because, of course, they are paid only when an author actually becomes published. So, when the first few agencies got back to me and, in a roundabout way, said, "Thanks, but no thanks," I wondered once again if my writing was actually ever going to get off the ground.

Why so many closed doors, God? I found myself thinking most mornings on my bike commute through leafy North Oxford springing to life again. *Is this not your will for me? Is this not your will for our life?*

———————— ❧ ————————

For many people, working at the Kilns would be just a job, nothing fancy about it. Of course, it was a quirky, old-fashioned house, which could be considered beautiful in and of itself. But it would still be just a job for folks who weren't as interested in C. S. Lewis. That was probably mostly true for Jen. And yet, it was something more, too.

Our first six months or so in Oxford were devastating for my wife. She had so much time to herself, so much time to sit and think about all of the "what ifs," all of the experiences she would now never be able to enjoy with her sister: summers at the lake,

Christmas morning with the family, the birth of our first child. I worried about Jen, and I often wondered if this was all worth it.

Because of Jen's struggles with grief and loneliness, her work at the Kilns was more than just a job. It helped us out financially, sure. But more importantly, it gave Jen reason and purpose for her time in Oxford. It was something of a psychological life raft.

Beyond answering emails and setting up tours, Jen would help Debbie organize paperwork and clean the Kilns. When I'd visit to give a tour, Debbie would tell me what a joy it was to have Jen at the house, what a lifesaver she was. "I know," I'd say with a smile, laughing to myself at the irony of it all. Jen's belief in me and this journey was enough to keep me going all those times I felt like throwing in the towel; Jen's presence at the Kilns made Debbie's job more manageable; and Debbie's offering her the job gave Jen reason to get out of bed in the morning.

My favorite days were when Jen didn't start her day at the Kilns until after lunch, and so she'd stop by Harris Manchester on her way, where I'd already been studying for some time, and we'd walk together down to the sandwich shop on the corner of Holywell Street and Mansfield Road. We'd order two chicken pesto paninis and eat them in the Harris Manchester gardens. We'd sit on a wood bench under a tree beside the chapel and eat with our eyes closed, faces tilted skyward. The spring sun would warm our faces as we enjoyed the crunchy bread and the gooey, hot cheese. Those were the good days.

Jane, our landlady in north Oxford, invited me over for tea one afternoon late that spring. Even though we were separated by nothing more than a hallway, I hardly saw her, given my study schedule and the fact that she was occupied with running her business, playing tennis with friends, ski trips in the Swiss Alps, and visits to London. She'd often be away for days at a time. When I did see her, she'd greet me with a smile as she hurried to her Mercedes, pulling out of the half-moon gravel driveway before I could even make it into the house. Because of our almost complete lack of interaction, her invitation to tea came as a surprise.

"Knock, knock," I said, miming a knock on the wood door as I opened it.

"Yes, hullo, Ryan," Jane's voice called from the kitchen. "Please come in."

Jane greeted me with the kind of smile that could sell toothpaste, with eyes like slivers and a posh, North-Oxford British accent. We made small talk for several minutes. She asked how my first year of studies had been, and I asked about Felix's sports and Dan's school. I'd ask a question, take a sip of tea, and listen, wondering how anyone could talk while holding that smile.

Eventually, Jane cut to the chase and told me that her parents' health was becoming a concern, and that they would, unfortunately, need the annex the following year. My stomach sunk.

I told her I was sorry we would not be returning, as we had enjoyed and appreciated our time in north Oxford. She told me they had enjoyed having us, and that she was happy they were able to have us so close for my first year of studies.

And so we would need to find a different place to live for my second year of studies. That is, of course, if we were even able to return for my second year.

Just before the end of my first year at Oxford, I heard back from a literary agent by the name of Amanda who was writing to say she had read my manuscript.

"I'm really drawn to your manuscript and your style," she wrote. "I think you connect with people very easily."

Amanda went on to say that she had some ideas on how to refine and repitch my manuscript to publishers.

"So, if you're interested in starting a conversation, let me know. I'd love for us to work together on this!"

I waited an agonizing half day, so as to play it cool, before writing back to say I'd be thrilled to work together.

June was our last month living in our North Oxford flat. Unfortunately, when the morning of June first rolled around, we did not have enough money in our bank account to cover our last month's rent.

Dreading Jane's look of frustration and impatience when I would have to ask her if we could have some more time to come up with rent, I left the house that morning in prayer that God might somehow help us cover our expenses, at least until we could get back to life in the States. I felt so irresponsible, not just for not having money to cover rent, but for not being able to take care of us.

Later that morning, Jen sent me an email while I was studying in the library. She wrote to tell me that the morning's mail— the mail arrives twice in England: once in the morning, and again in the afternoon—had brought a letter from some of our family back home. Apparently, someone had been thinking of us and felt led to send us some extra money, hoping it might be of help.

I paid Jane our rent when I returned home that evening. Afterward, we had £15 left in our bank account.

─────────────────── ❧ ───────────────────

Jen was waving good-bye to me from her seat in the back row of a bus the last time I saw her in Oxford that spring. I watched the bus pull out of the Gloucester Green bus station, standing there for several long seconds with my hands in my pockets, before cycling to Harris Manchester. Taking a seat at my desk beside the second-story windows that face North Oxford and those passing along Mansfield Road, I found myself missing her already.

I remained in England for a few weeks to finish my term's work while Jen returned to the States early to attend my sister's high school graduation. Since my studies meant I could not be there for my sister, we thought it best if Jen went.

My sister and I do not share the same father. Nor, in fact, do my brother and I. But she is my sister, and he is my brother, and it has always been so. No "steps" about it.

My sister and I are a lot alike. My mother writes me from time to time to tell me about something my sister has done, or a face she made, or something she said. About how it reminds her of me.

We share the same lanky frame, and we both do pretty well for ourselves in school. Growing up in what was most often a single-parent household, with the three of us and my mother, and nearly eight years separating my younger sister and me, I was something like a father to her. Whereas she and my brother were close enough to have their spats, ours was a different relationship. Less bickering, more protecting. More advice, too, I suppose.

I am not sure whether or not I have ever shared this story with her, but one of the memories of my sister that stands out in my mind is from the very first few years of her life. We were in the woods behind our house at the time, and my mom had allowed us to play outside on our own.

In what was admittedly one of my worst ideas, I spotted a large stump on the hill on which I thought we might sit together. I carried her to it and then lifted her up onto its fluffy, mossy surface, before pulling myself up. The stump looked out over the hill, over our double-wide trailer, and the thickly wooded forest. The hill was steep enough that the drop on the opposite side from which we climbed was several lengths of my body. Shortly after I took my seat atop the stump beside my baby sister, I found myself looking around the forest only to return my gaze to her just in time to see her begin to careen backward over the edge of the stump. In a flash, I grabbed the front of her shirt just before she was lost to sight, returning her to her upright position. My heart nearly beat its way out of my chest, and my little-boy mind was sure in that moment that, had I not caught her, she would not have survived the fall. From our seat atop this mossy stump, I held her close and told her how sorry I was.

Many years later, when she was in high school, I held my sister close once again, her head buried in my shoulder, tears wetting my shirt. We stood in the middle of a dingy motel room, where she and her father had been staying while he was visiting from out of state. Her clothes filled a black, plastic garbage sack at our feet; an old television and mini fridge sat on the opposite side of the room from two twin beds. A ceiling fan hung heavy and still overhead.

As I held her there, a police car pulled around the side of the motel, under the streetlamps and rain, before carrying her father off to prison. He had a warrant out for his arrest and it had caught up with him.

We stood there for several long, quiet minutes, her sobs muffled in my shoulder, the only sound that broke the silence. My eyes stayed on one of the lampshades hanging from the wall, a brown stain on one of its sides. I held my sister tightly until I extended my arms so I could look her in her eyes.

"Let's go home."

I did not realize how bad it would hurt, my not being there for her graduation, until it was too late.

Soon, she would be preparing to leave for college, and as she strode across that graduation stage at my old high school, surrounded by cornfields and dairy farms and the inevitable smell of fertilizer, she stopped to thank me for showing her the way. Once again, questions made their home in the back of my mind as I tried to study, wondering whether or not this journey would ever prove to be worth all that it had meant I would miss.

One of the perks of being president of the Oxford University C. S. Lewis Society is that I had the opportunity to treat the weekly speakers to dinner beforehand. Walter would often join us, along with one or two other regular society members. Sometimes Jen would come along, too, which made things seem complete.

We would often meet at a cramped, family-owned French restaurant on Little Clarendon Street in the city center—more a narrow alley than a street, with Christmas lights zigzagging overhead year-round. It was Walter's favorite.

"You know they only use fresh ingredients here?" Walter would say, without fail, as we read the menu. He loved to tell the story about running into the owner in the city center one day and asking what he would be serving the following night, when Walter had dinner reservations.

"Tomorrow night?" the restaurant owner asked. "Why, I am on my way to the market now to find out what they have on hand for me to serve tonight. How should I know what I will serve *tomorrow* night?!"

While the society meetings were often quite full, these intimate dinner conversations were a good opportunity to get to know the speakers, and to hear longer stories they might not have time to share during their presentation.

One of my favorite dinners was with Laurence Harwood, C. S. Lewis's godson. Laurence was tall and well dressed. He spoke in a calm voice, which peaked to excited high notes when he recalled what it was like to grow up with Lewis visiting his family home for dinner and conversations with his parents.

"I always loved it when Jack came around," Laurence told us. "As children, we'd be playing games when he'd come over, and he'd get right down there with us on the floor, at our level. He was genuinely interested in what we were playing, and he'd play with us. Not in a condescending way. He'd always beat us, of course, but we really enjoyed him."

Laurence told us Lewis never pushed his own Christian faith on him. He told us how, even as a child, Lewis never bought him a book on Christianity or even religion in general, to try to influence what he should believe.

"Even though that was his role, as my godfather."

He told us about the many letters Lewis wrote, and said he figured Lewis must have written more than two hundred thousand during his lifetime. Laurence told us that Lewis would often spend two to three hours a day responding to those who wrote him, as he felt it was only right that he reply to anyone who took the time to send him a letter. He recalled that Lewis would often include illustrations in the letters he wrote to Laurence and other children, at those times when it might help to picture a certain point he was making. If, for example, Lewis wrote to tell Laurence about a book he was writing that had a bear in it, he'd draw a picture of a bear. Or, in a letter at the end of December, he'd include a sketch of himself sitting down to eat the Christmas turkey dinner he had written about. Not in the margin, but right in the middle of the paragraph. Laurence told us how, as a child, he looked forward to receiving these letters, and how delightfully odd it seemed to him as an adult that this was the same, brilliant Oxford and Cambridge don who spent his time reading and teaching medieval literature.

Before the meal was finished, Laurence shared a trying experience he faced during his own days as an Oxford student. He told us how, after being struck with double pneumonia, he did not pass his first-year's preliminary exams, and was not able to return for his second year. He received a letter from Lewis in response to hearing this news.

"At the moment, I can well imagine, everything seems in ruins," Lewis wrote to Laurence. "That is an illusion."

Lewis encouraged his godson neither to dwell on this seemingly bad news, nor to consider himself the victim of Oxford's exam system, but rather to do his best to brush himself off and get on with life. He must trust that this would actually serve to save him much hard work and many years spent traveling in what very well might have been the wrong direction. Lewis went on to explain that many people, if not most, find this to be one of life's most difficult periods, struggling from failure to failure, as it had been for him.

> Life consisted of applying for jobs which other people got, writing books that no one would publish and giving lectures that no one attended. It all looks hopelessly hopeless, yet the vast majority of us manage to get on somehow and shake down somewhere in the end. You are now going through what most people (at least most of the people I know) find, in retrospect to have been the most unpleasant period of their lives.
>
> But it won't last; the road usually improves later. I think life is rather like a bumpy bed in a bad hotel. At first you can't imagine how you can lie on it, much less sleep on it. But presently one finds the right position and finally one is snoring away. By the time one is called it seems a very good bed and one is loath to leave it. (*C. S. Lewis, My Godfather* 125)

I said good-bye to Cole from Oxford that spring. He had been offered an unconditional spot to do his PhD work in Scotland—which meant he had a place waiting for him no matter how he did on his exams—and he would be moving over the summer. One of the last times I saw him before he left was at the Ashmolean Museum, in the city center. He surprised me with a small, gift-wrapped box. Tearing back the wrapping paper, I let out a shocked "No way!" in a volume that was not museum friendly.

The faded, gold lettering on the blue spine read *Mere Christianity*.

"It's a first edition," Cole said proudly. "I found it at St. Phillip's."

He grinned as if he had just hit the game-winning homerun. It would be nearly a full year before I saw Cole again.

Not knowing whether it would be my last term in Oxford or not, I did my best to do as many of those things I'd longed to experience but had never had time for before. One of those was waking up early to attend Friday morning chapel at my college.

Unlike many of the other Oxford colleges, Harris Manchester's chapel is not all that impressive. Other college chapels have ceilings that shoot high into the air and are built with enough arched stone and stained glass to fill most churches ten times over. Harris Manchester's chapel is smaller, with a lower wood ceiling and forward-facing pews, all of which feels not unlike a local parish.

The sound of an organ told me I had arrived just as the service began. The room was dim, and the officiant standing behind the lectern, wearing a black robe and a rather serious face, spoke slowly and deliberately.

After welcoming the few of us in this otherwise empty chapel, he began with a reading from the Old Testament. He read the story of God's conversation with Moses in the book of Exodus, the story of Moses's calling. The story tells about the time when God spoke to Moses from a flaming bush that, curiously, did not burn up, when God told Moses he would rescue God's people from their Egyptian captivity and lead his people out of Egypt.

From his position behind the lectern, with only a hint of light on his face, the man in the front of the chapel read about how Moses responded not with pride and expectation, but with fear and confusion.

"But I am nobody," Moses says in response, wondering why in the world God would use *him* of all people for such an incredible mission. Of course, it was precisely because Moses was a nobody that God had chosen Moses.

Moses was right. He was a nobody. A baby found in a basket floating down the Nile. A murderer, even, who had fled Egypt fearing for his life. And now, a shepherd, who spent his days alone with his thoughts and a bunch of animals. And because of this, there could be no confusion as to who was responsible for Israel's salvation: not the one who was called, but, rather, the One who called.

We sang several hymns that morning, which made the small chapel come alive and suddenly appear much bigger than it had before. The man in the dark robe returned to the lectern for a short reading before the close of the service. The lectern lamp once again lit his face slightly, and this time I could almost swear he wore the hint of a smile as he gave the benediction:

May the peace of the Lord Christ go with you,
wherever he may send you.
May he guide you through the wilderness,
protect you through the storm.
May he bring you home rejoicing
at the wonders he has shown you.

> May he bring you home rejoicing
> once again into our doors.

The night before I was due to leave England, Debbie phoned and asked if I might like to spend my last evening in Oxford at the Kilns. There was, of course, only one answer to such a question. As if that weren't enough, Debbie told me that, while guests aren't typically allowed to stay in Lewis's old room, that she would make an exception in my case.

I fell asleep in Lewis's old bedroom, wondering to myself whether this would be the last of my days in this most incredible city, and praying to God that it would not.

8

Identity

Who You Are, Not What You Do

The San Juan Islands are one of the best-kept secrets in America. Of course, the Pacific Northwest is my home, so I am biased, but I struggle to think of many other places I'd rather be. Particularly in the summer.

Just south of Vancouver and a couple hours northwest of Seattle lies a sprinkling of small islands, where God long ago dredged his fingers through the earth and formed it like clay, allowing the great waters to wash in and fill the void. The islands look like green porcupines floating face down in the water; they are covered by evergreen trees that, silhouetted against a tangerine sunset or sunrise, are one of my favorite sights in the world. During the day, deer roam the island freely, waves lap the rocky shoreline, and sailboats and orca whales dance on the horizon. At night, the stars hang so low and bright that, when you lie on your back gazing up, you begin to lose yourself in them, and you do not move for fear you might fall into the deep blue starry sea overhead, casting a cosmic splash in all directions.

Not long after I returned to the States, I filled a backpack with some clothes, a towel, a small tent, and a journal, and caught a ferry to Orcas Island, one of the hundreds of islands that make up the San Juans. Before leaving Oxford, in a funny coincidence, I met a middle-aged man from Orcas Island. He wore a black leather bracelet and a scruffy beard with hints of gray revealing his age. "I'm Dick," he said, grasping my hand in a firm hand-shake, before telling me about his studies at Harvard and pastoring a church in New England. For many years, he had been a nationally syndicated radio talk-show host out of Chicago, where he spent his days reading books and interviewing all sorts of writers. He's now retired and lives with his wife on Orcas Island in Washington State. Dick had been passing through Oxford when our paths crossed. He stopped at the Kilns for a quick visit at the same time I dropped in to make sure I wasn't needed for a tour.

When Dick heard that I was from Washington State, and that I would be back in the Pacific Northwest for the summer, he told me about the retreat he hosts each year for Christian artists. "Artists of all types," he told me. Some in film, some in photography. Lots of writers and musicians. All of them gather together on Orcas Island in the model of Lewis and Tolkien and the rest of the Inklings of Oxford, to encourage one another, to journey together, and to create the kind of music and paintings and stories that point to God's unique work of healing this wounded, broken world. The kind of work that will be enjoyed not only by fellow Christians, but by people from different faiths or no faith at all.

From our seats on wood stools in the Kilns' kitchen that June afternoon, with sunlight pouring in and the garden in full bloom framed by the kitchen windows, Dick told me about how he had become a Christian in the Bay Area in the 1960s. And it showed. Though he was clearly well-read and witty, he used the words "dude" and "man," and he sounded, at times, like a dead ringer for Jeff Bridges' character from the film, *The Big Lebowski*. He sounded like "The Dude."

A man named Nigel joined Dick at the Kilns that afternoon. To this day, I am not sure I have ever met a man who dresses with as much flair and style as Nigel. He wore a purple and white striped shirt tucked into his pants, with the sleeves rolled up to his elbows and the collar standing on end, with brightly colored socks to match. His graying hair was nearly as big as his character, rising high above his head, somehow without seeming out of control. Nigel told me that he had been a stage actor in London, and how he had studied at L'Abri with Francis Schaeffer.

There are certain people you meet in life who seem to be operating on a different plane than the rest of us. While the rest of us are running scared for our lives, as if our hair were on fire, they are strolling with their hands in their pockets, whistling, and smiling. Nigel is one of those people.

"Tell me your story, Ryan," Nigel said in a quiet, serious voice from his seat on the stool across the cramped kitchen, sipping the hot tea he cupped in his hands. He listened with narrowed eyes and a lowered brow. He'd ask questions every so often. Great questions. But mostly he listened.

As it turns out, I wasn't needed for the tour that day.

"See ya on Orcas," Dick said in his Dude-like voice as we said good-bye from the Kilns, wearing a sideways grin, clasping my hand in his and shaking it firmly.

It was late July when I stepped off the ferry on Orcas Island. I made a phone call to track down a cab that would take me to the small town where the retreat was being held, on the opposite side of the island. The woman on the line told me my cab would be there to pick me up in five minutes or so. Less than a minute later, an old Mercedes pulled up and a man with long, dark hair, dressed in a black T-shirt and blue jeans, leaned over to the passenger window.

"Heading to Eastsound?"

"Uh, yeah," I said, still unsure if this was my ride.

"Well, hop in," he said, before getting out and helping me load my bags into the trunk. He waved me to the passenger door. Two small dogs were sitting in the front: one in his seat, one in mine.

"They don't bite," he reassured me, squeezing behind the steering wheel and pointing to the long-haired brown dog closest to me, "But he'll probably want to sit in your lap."

He did.

We were less than a half mile down the narrow road, with evergreens standing like giants on each side of the car, when my driver pulled a joint out of the glove box and began lighting up, holding the steering wheel between his knees.

He took a long puff, squeezing his cheeks in for a few moments, before blowing it out the window and extending his arm to offer me a hit.

"Oh, no thanks," I told him, trying to hide my disbelief, still wondering what kind of taxi service this was.

He didn't seem bothered. Returning the joint to his lips, he used a now-free hand to turn up the stereo.

"Do you like the Floyd?" he asked between pursed lips and intent eyes, as if this was a matter of great importance. And here's the thing, if you ever find yourself getting a ride with a stranger—who may or may not actually be a taxi driver—who proceeds to light a joint and ask if you like "the Floyd," you say yes. Always. Even if you are only half-certain he's referring to the band Pink Floyd. Even if you have never heard of the band Pink Floyd and could not pick them out if you tried.

"The Floyd?" I asked. "Yeah, love 'em."

I wish I knew his name, but there was no name tag on his baggy T-shirt. He wasn't wearing anything at all that led me to believe he was actually a taxi driver.

After we agreed that the Floyd is one of the greatest rock bands of all time, he proceeded to tell me he's been a millionaire several times over, and how he lost it all each time.

"Isn't that just how it goes?" he asked, still holding the joint between his lips.

The view on either side of the road opened up and we could now see the island's rolling, green fields. He waved his hand to the homes standing on top of the hills and told me about the retired CIA agents who live all over the islands. He also told me that he was certain aliens were controlling the world through a small, elite group of powerful men.

I reached into my pocket and pulled out some cash to pay him when he stopped the car, but he extended a hand to stop me.

"It's on the house."

Such was my introduction to Orcas Island.

After dropping my things off at a makeshift campsite that had been set up next to a white church that looked like it was straight out of a Norman Rockwell painting, I wandered into the small, waterfront town. The air smelled salty, and seagulls hung over the water as if suspended from the clouds. I found Dick mingling in a crowd of people in a building overlooking the harbor.

"Hey, man!" Dick said with a loud voice and wide smile, before wrapping me in a bear hug. "I met this guy at C. S. Lewis's house!" Dick told the people with whom he had been talking, pointing to me with his thumb. After asking about my trip, Dick introduced me to several people standing nearby, mostly middle-aged artist types—old friends of Dick's, I assumed. It was the first time I had ever been around so many talented, successful artists who were also Christians. The people there were dressed in a way that made me suddenly feel terribly out of place. Men in sweaters and dress shirts. A few ties. Women in dresses and at least one faux fur neck warmer. I wore a T-shirt, cargo pants, and Vans.

One morning that week, I was eating at a bed-and-breakfast that overlooked the ocean when a couple invited me to join them at their table. Not recognizing me, they rightly assumed it was my first time there. They were around my parents' age, and they asked what had brought me to the conference. I explained about running into Nigel and Dick at the Kilns and that my wife and I were from the area. They told me they were old friends of Dick's from their time together in Chicago.

I asked what they did, and the husband replied with a question of his own.

"Have you heard of the *Halo* video game series?"

"Yes, of course."

"I composed the soundtrack for it," he told me. "Among other things."

"Oh," I said, taking a drink of my orange juice to cover up my being at a loss for words.

Later on in the week, I met a photographer who told me stories from her time with bands like Nirvana and Soundgarden and Pearl Jam, about how wild Seattle was back in the '90s, during the heyday of grunge rock.

The church next to the campsite, which was now crowded with photographers, musicians, and writers, was done up inside to resemble the Eagle & Child pub in Oxford, complete with a chalkboard menu. The walls of the church were adorned with paintings from artists attending the retreat.

From this makeshift pub, Dick gave a short talk to kick off the gathering. One of the things he liked to mention was the idea that we come from many different backgrounds and experience, but that we all have something to contribute: a bit of fish, or a piece of bread, which isn't so special on its own. "But together," Dick said, "God intends to make of it a feast."

At night, we'd gather around a bonfire on a hill overlooking the crescent-shaped bay, and people would take turns sharing their work while children roasted marshmallows and deer wandered through the apple orchard in the twilight background. Nigel emceed the evenings, standing beside the fire holding a tall walking stick someone had given him, and looking very much like Gandalf (minus the beard and hat).

My friend Freya, whom I had only just met, told us about how she had prayed for a cello for years. Looking down at the cello in her hands, she shared the story of how someone had recently told her they had a cello they felt like God wanted them to give to her. Beside the fire that night was the first time she played her cello in public, ice-skating her way through the notes. When she was done, the applause roared, and she walked away with an ear-to-ear smile on her face, her new cello in hand. Authors dressed in turtlenecks and wearing thick-rimmed glasses read from their books; a twentysomething opera singer from Toronto peeled back the night air and made the hair on the back of my neck stand on end; and children took a break from roasting marshmallows to read the poetry they had written, or to provide interpretive dance to someone's song. All of it came together in such a breathtaking way. It was like coming home, to a home I never knew existed.

The night before I left Orcas Island, I sat around a table in a hotel restaurant overlooking the ocean, with a handful of new friends. We were talking about what we intended to take away from our time together, as well as what we were hoping to do or accomplish.

One young guy from California mentioned that he realized it was time for him to stop taking time for granted and to start taking his music more seriously. He told us all he was finally going to set out on tour. "To setting out on tour," someone said, the sound of glasses clinking around the table providing an exclamation point to the sentence.

My friend Freya mentioned that she was going to stop worrying about whether her cello talents were "good enough" or not. And that she was really only interested in playing for an audience of One. "To an audience of One!" Glasses clinked around the table. The rockstar photographer said this time had reminded her, even though she had been struggling lately, with many tears spilt on her pillow, that we worship a God who turns mourning into dancing, and that it was time she lived that reality. "To mourning into dancing!" More glasses clinked.

And then it was my turn.

With my eyes glued to the base of the glass directly in front of me, I told the group I had been working on a writing project for some time. I told them it was something I was hoping might one day be published, but that I was having a tough time with it, and that I was feeling unsure whether or not that was actually the path for me. I confessed that I felt uncomfortable even admitting that I wanted to be a writer, not yet having a book published, but that, in a strange way, this time on the Island had encouraged me that I was supposed to be writing.

The woman to my right, who created gorgeous handmade earrings and bracelets and all kinds of funky jewelry, made a confused face. Like I had just posed a calculus problem to the group.

"Ryan, writing isn't something you do or don't do," she said. "Writing is who you *are*."

In that moment, I felt as though I could finally take off all my silly clothes, clothes fashioned out of some hope of fitting into others' expectations, and simply be who I am.

"You're a writer, Ryan," she told me with a reassuring, confident smile and a nod. Those words made me breathe a sigh of relief. I was twenty-six when I realized: I am a writer.

Jen will of course remind me at this point that she told me this years ago. And she's right. She did tell me I'm meant to be a writer, years before I ever felt comfortable admitting it and long before anyone else noticed. But anyone with a spouse will know what I mean when I say sometimes we have to hear it from someone else before it becomes true for us.

I left Orcas Island with new friends and newfound confidence. I left knowing it was time to take my writing more seriously. Not because it was so great, but because I came to learn that it is somehow a part of who I am. That, in a strange way, it reveals something of God's fingerprint on my life. As Dick liked to say, because it may only be some bits of fish, or a handful of breadcrumbs, but it is what I could contribute to the great feast God is preparing.

I hadn't yet unpacked my bags from England when I received a note from someone in Washington State who knew I had recently returned from England and who was familiar with our journey. He was not, however, aware of our financial struggles or our prayers for a miracle. No one knew about that. Not my parents. Not Jen's. No one.

Knowing we'd just returned, he wrote to tell me he was hoping we could meet. He said he had something he wanted to tell me, and that he'd prefer to do it in person.

After a bit of small talk, he told me that he wanted me to know that I did not have to worry about where the money was going to come from for our second year in Oxford. I felt the hair on my arms stand on end, and tears welled in my eyes. He went on to tell me that he wanted to take care of this for us. That he wanted to take care of all of it.

I didn't know what to say; I didn't know what to do. Streaking tears soon warmed my cheeks. They were, in that moment, the only words I had.

I called Jen on the drive home. I couldn't wait to tell her. Nor could she believe it. We'd be returning to Oxford for my second year after all, and I would be able to finish what I had started. Though we still had no idea where we'd be living when we did.

As it turns out, finding a place to live in Oxford is ridiculously competitive. Apparently, students line up outside of the real estate offices before they even open their doors at the start of each month, just to get a chance to see what's newly available. Most times, housing available for the fall is already snatched up the spring before, which made it very difficult for us to find a place that summer. From Washington State, no less.

With less than a month before we were scheduled to leave, friends at church would ask if we had found a place to live yet.

"No, not yet," I'd say.

"Well, it will work out," they'd say, doing their best to encourage us. But we were beginning to get worried.

Two weeks before we flew out, I received an email from Debbie.

"I know how strange this is going to sound," she began. "But there is an extra room available at the Kilns that the Foundation would like to fill."

Debbie told me that she didn't know whether we had already found something or not, or whether we'd even be open to the idea of living there at the Kilns, along with her and a recently graduated Oxford student named Jonathan.

"But if you're interested, we'd love to have you both live with us here."

Called

With that, we were ready for our return to England, and our second year in Oxford.

9

Unanswered Prayers

When all the doors closed

"You know what returning to Oxford is like for me?" my friend, Professor Steve, asked over lunch at the Eagle & Child pub one sunny spring afternoon. Leaning across the thick, wood table to complete his sentence, his voice quieted to a near whisper. "It's like returning to Narnia."

His hushed voice revealed this full-grown man's embarrassment at his confession. A smile spread slowly across his face, like a child remembering the smell of cookies in his grandmother's kitchen. Or being struck in a moment of joy by the memory of a magical dream he had once.

I think Professor Steve was right. Returning to Oxford *was* a bit like returning to Narnia. When I had said good-bye the previous spring, I did not know whether I would be returning. And part of me shuddered at the thought of Oxford and our first year in this incredible city becoming no more than the dream of a distant land I once visited, but now could only vaguely recall in flashes and smoke before I lost it completely.

It was a little like returning to a dream, and with it all the rush of excitement at the familiar joy and peace it brings: the sound of so many different accents floating by as your bike bounces over cobblestones in the city center; a hot cup of midday tea savored at the second-story desk in the library while the rain beats down on the windows and the umbrellas of those shuffling by on the street below; the alluring, dusty smell that only comes from old books; and all of the familiar faces this place brought, now returned. Not unlike a dream, I suppose. Certainly not unlike returning to Narnia, when, at your worst moments, you were growing ever more certain you might never return.

We moved into C. S. Lewis's former home that autumn. Debbie had set aside Lewis's brother's former room for us near the rear of the house, beside the library. We loaded our clothes into an old wardrobe that opened to reveal a vertical mirror, space to hang clothes, and shelves labeled by brass nameplates that read, "neckties," "socks," and the like. A short, skinny vase holding wildflowers was placed on a wide, wood desk that sat just beneath a window looking out at the garden, and a wingback chair stood beside a small nightstand in the corner of the room.

The perfect spot for reading, I thought.

Jonathan, a thirtysomething who had recently finished his doctorate in Classics at Oxford, joined Debbie, Jen, and me at the Kilns. Jonathan had also been leading tours the year before, so both Jen and I knew him when we moved in.

As far as I can gather, Jonathan came from a privileged family, though he never talked much about it. Both he and his brother attended a prep school not far from London, and they both later went to Oxford. Jonathan has a tall, lanky frame, which he uses not for sport, but for dressing sharply and reading books. He has a posh British accent, and while he is incredibly humble, he is one of the most intelligent people I have ever met.

Jonathan and I quickly became like brothers, throwing verbal jabs at one another and sharing late-night conversations, sometimes around the pond, sometimes from the front room. He had a stereotypically dry sense of humor, which I loved. He once remarked that my jokes were best described as superfluous. I laughed out loud. Then, when I had thought about it for a moment, I realized he was probably right. Sharing the house with Jonathan and Debbie was no small addition to the gift of living at the Kilns.

The Kilns is three miles from the Oxford city center. Three miles uphill, if you're traveling to the Kilns, which makes for an exhausting bike ride after studying all day. But when you're just starting your day, I found the three-mile downhill ride provides a good early morning wake-up, with rain pelting your face in tiny pinpricks until it's numb, and your hair blowing back as if in a wind tunnel.

There was a bus that ran from the Kilns to the city center, which I would take from time to time, but mostly I biked. After sitting in the library all day, I figured it would be good to use my legs a bit.

Jonathan also made the daily commute to Oxford's city center to teach, choosing to forego not only the bus, but also a bicycle. He would walk the three-mile trip to the city center each morning, and then back again in the evening. During his life at the Kilns, C. S. Lewis would also walk the three-mile trip to the city center, and Magdalene College, where he taught. During the afternoon, he often enjoyed a break from writing and teaching by strolling Addison's Walk, the leafy, dirt foot trail that follows the River Cherwell around the college grounds, before walking home in the evenings. Perhaps walking was Jonathan's way of stepping into the shoes of the man in whose home he now lived. Debbie figured Jonathan was simply too posh to ride the bus. Personally, I preferred the bike ride.

First down Kilns Lane, a narrow road that passed through the small village of Risinghurst, with tiny cars parked on either side of the already cramped road. Past a row of shops, with workers getting ready for the day: two small grocery stores, several banks, a real estate office, and several restaurants. I got used to seeing the owner of the fish-and-chips shop cleaning up from the night before, sweeping the front sidewalk, or prepping for the day in the kitchen when I rode past.

Then came the prep school where Emma Watson attended before she became known as "Hermione," and Oxford-Brooks University, which was a trade school before becoming a university. The "other" Oxford university, if I can put it that way.

Then down the steep Headington Hill, which overlooked the city center, adjacent to South Parks, where Guy Fawkes Day was celebrated each autumn. Past another string of shops, through a roundabout, and then, finally, over Magdalene Bridge, where the view opened up to the High Street, and the heart of Oxford's city center, with tall colleges looming like castles on either side of the street. The view of Magdalene Bridge passing over the River Cherwell, where students and tourists and families traveled on punts in the spring, filled me with joy each morning.

Of course, the ride home was reversed, with the long, low-grade hill of Kilns Lane providing one last challenge before making it home each evening, with just enough energy to slump into bed at the end of a long day.

At the foot of Kilns Lane stood something I never would have expected to find in Oxford. Disguised among a row of native trees was a very non-native palm tree. There it stood on the corner, in front of a plain-looking house, pretending as though it was at home in this small Oxford village. Standing there tall and quiet and still, doing its best not to be noticed. Hoping someone wouldn't realize it had no right to be in a place like Oxford, and promptly remove it.

The first time I saw it, riding home to the Kilns one night, I had to do a double take.

"A palm tree in Oxford," I thought to myself, looking back over my shoulder at the tree. "How curious."

———————— ❧ ————————

Not long into my second year, I heard from Amanda, my literary agent. She wrote to ask if we could Skype. She had some good news to share.

"So, our hard work this summer paid off," she said from my laptop in the front room of the Kilns. She was referring to the rewrites we had collaborated on.

Amanda told me she had sent out my revised manuscript proposal and that it had been well received by a number of publishers. In fact, she told me there was one publisher who liked it so much they were hoping to have a call with me to get to know me a bit better.

Around ten o'clock one night, about a week later and after a long day of studies, I had my Skype call with this publisher. Two guys were on the call: one young, around my age, the other about ten years older. One was the editor, the other the head of acquisitions.

Not wasting any time, they started the call by saying they had enjoyed my manuscript, which helped settle the butterflies stirring in my belly. They went on to say they were hoping to have a chance to get to know me a bit better as they considered my project.

"This could take ten minutes, or it could take thirty minutes, we'll just see how it goes," the younger one said.

About an hour later, they thanked me for taking the time to chat, and told me that they would be in touch with their decision in a of couple weeks.

"I am not sure that could have gone any better," I said to Jen, who had been in the room for the call, with a look of relief after closing my laptop on my desk. Jen agreed. We both figured anything but good news would be a surprise.

Holy Trinity Church is a small Anglican parish so hidden by trees and homes you might not find it if you didn't know it was there. Bordered on one side by woods and a leafy foot trail, and a row of quaint, old English homes on the other, Holy Trinity is not so out of the ordinary as far as English churches go. It is, however, unique in that it is where C. S. Lewis attended church for most of his adult life. It is also where he is buried.

What surprised me most when I first visited Holy Trinity is that there were no neon signs. There was a small, inconspicuous sign at one end of the graveyard, pointing in the general direction of Lewis's headstone. But that was all. If the graveyard where Lewis is buried were in the States, there would most certainly be a neon sign, likely with "L-E-W-I-S V-E-G-A-S" in giant, blinking letters.

Inside, a framed photo of C. S. Lewis hung in the back of the church, and one of the windows was etched with an illustration of several of the children and animals from the Narnia chronicles. There was also a tiny, unassuming bronze plaque on the pew where Lewis used to sit, on the left side of the sanctuary, beside a marble column that very nearly blocked the view of the pulpit. It seemed to me a rather unfortunate seat. I liked to imagine he came in late to church one morning, breathing a bit heavy from the walk, found this to be the only remaining seat, and spent the rest of his Sunday mornings there. I pictured Lewis sitting beside old women in long, thick dresses; children being hushed by their parents; and old men falling asleep in tweed jackets, all while he struggled to see the vicar deliver the morning's sermon.

The church was filled with many of the same sorts of characters I imagine Lewis found himself seated beside in his own day when Jen and I attended Holy Trinity one Sunday morning that autumn: mothers with busy children, grey-haired women, and men with cowlicks in the same tweed jackets they'd been wearing for decades. The officiants wore white robes, and a handful of men and women made up the choir, all coming to the front of the church in a line led by someone carrying a cross on a tall, golden pole. The last person in the line was a vicar who wore a long, blonde ponytail that fell neatly across his white-robed shoulders.

After a few hymns, the vicar read a passage from Scripture that spoke of finishing a race strong. He asked all of us seated there that morning to picture ourselves finishing a race. He asked us to picture ourselves in a stadium, overflowing with all of the saints from history, who were there cheering us on.

At first, I found myself cold to the idea of being the center of such attention, as though the saints had nothing better to do than to cheer for me. But then, somewhere in between the time he started and the time we left the church that morning, I was swept up in it all. I couldn't help but feel as though maybe there was something to all of this. Maybe there was something to seeing yourself as part of a movement bigger than yourself, and not merely on an island, trying to go it alone.

I had been feeling exhausted for some time, trying to go it on my own in my studies and in my writing. I also felt removed from the world, being so far from home, spending all my waking hours with my nose in a book or Greek flash cards, and having little time to invest in community since arriving in Oxford.

Maybe there was something to seeing yourself as somehow part of this long tradition of women and men who have come before us, as part of what Paul calls the very body of Christ, alive and at work in the world. Not merely made up of those who happen to be alive when we are, but across history, separated by centuries and oceans and even languages.

Maybe there was something to this idea of being cheered on by those who have come before us, by those who have run the race and who have finished strong. Encouraging us to keep going, whether all the doors seem to be closing or we find before us only open doors.

"Keep going," the ponytailed vicar said that morning with a smile, the late morning sun now pouring in from the windows behind him at the front of the church. "Finish strong."

Cynical though I had been when he started painting this picture, I left Holy Trinity that morning with fresh air in my lungs and new life in my legs.

"Keep going," his words echoed in my ears. I smiled and curled my fingers around Jen's hand as we made our way past Lewis's headstone, through the narrow church gate, down the village lane, and back to the home that sits at the end of Lewis Close.

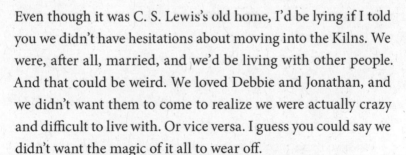

Even though it was C. S. Lewis's old home, I'd be lying if I told you we didn't have hesitations about moving into the Kilns. We were, after all, married, and we'd be living with other people. And that could be weird. We loved Debbie and Jonathan, and we didn't want them to come to realize we were actually crazy and difficult to live with. Or vice versa. I guess you could say we didn't want the magic of it all to wear off.

But it didn't. We loved living with Debbie and Jonathan at the Kilns. Mostly it was just the four of us there, though we'd sometimes have short-term guests. Usually, our guests were North American scholars on sabbatical, escaping their busy routine to get some writing done at the Kilns. One time it was a philosopher from Dallas who had won a book-of-the-year award a few years earlier and was now working on a screenplay. Another time it was an English professor from North Carolina who was writing a book on Joy Davidman, the New Yorker C. S. Lewis married late in life. But most of the time, it was just the four of us.

I came home after a long day at college one evening, the pebble walkway crunching underfoot as I approached the front door, when I stopped suddenly. Looking into the kitchen, the light from which illuminated the darkness in which I stood outside, I saw Jen and Debbie preparing dinner, both smiling. Debbie was laughing. Because they didn't know I was there, I was able to simply see how happy they both were, without interrupting. It was as though God was putting a hand on my shoulder for a moment and saying, "Wait. Just wait. Wait right here. I want you to have a look at this. I want you to see that *I* am taking care of things. Everything will be all right."

Debbie became like a second mom to me. She would often make soup during the cold autumn days, and she'd always make sure I knew I could help myself to the leftovers in the fridge. She also baked the most incredible oatmeal raisin cookies—my favorite—which would fill the home with smells of cinnamon and roasted oats. She'd make a huge batch and keep them in Tupperware on the kitchen counter for us. I'd often grab a couple and take them to bed with me at the end of a long day, eating one as I walked barefoot across the cold, uneven hardwood floors to our rooms in the rear of the house.

I'd spend most of the week studying at college in the city center, returning home in time for dinner with Jen. Most days, Jen would spend her time at the Kilns, helping Debbie arrange tours and prepare teas for guests. On the nights I dined with the speaker for that week's C. S. Lewis Society meeting, Jen would often join me in town for dinner. On Friday nights, Jen would usually take the bus to the city center and I would meet her for dinner in celebration of another week's worth of studies complete. And sometimes, when we were feeling particularly aristocratic, we'd spring for a movie, and then we'd spend our bus ride back to the Kilns discussing the characters and story. Or we'd take a seat on the old brick bench beside the pond just beyond the Kilns, and we'd talk late into the night. Those were my favorite times.

"Does it blow you away to think that the same constellations you find in the sky back home in Washington you can also pick out here, halfway around the world, in England?" I asked Jen as we approached the Kilns late one evening after a date night in the city center, with my neck craned, and my eyes fixed on the stars overhead.

Jen paused for a moment. "No, because I don't look for constellations in the States, and I don't look for them here," she said, searching her pockets for her keys. "I look where I'm going, rather than staring up at the stars."

"Is that a metaphor?" I asked, still gazing skyward, as Jen found her keys and used them to open the door.

"No, it's just what I do," she said with a hint of impatience.

"I think it's a metaphor," I said, scraping the wet leaves from my shoes on the door frame before following her inside.

Debbie doesn't eat meat. Which made the scene of her cleaning a giant, pink-and-white raw turkey in the Kilns kitchen so funny.

Three of the four of us living at the Kilns were from the States, so we decided a proper American Thanksgiving was necessary. The thing was, none of us had ever prepared a turkey before. Except for the vegetarian, before she was a vegetarian.

"This just goes to show how much I love you guys," Debbie said, laughing, with her hand reaching deep inside the turkey.

It was the eve of Thanksgiving, and the three of us were in the kitchen preparing for our meal together the next day. Jen helped Debbie prepare the turkey, and I sat on a stool chopping carrots and celery.

When Debbie and Jen finished preparing the turkey, Debbie retired for the evening, leaving just Jen and me in the kitchen.

I was still chopping vegetables when I found my thoughts wandering to how incredible this whole scene was. I was now in my second year of studies at Oxford, preparing for Thanksgiving with Jen at C. S. Lewis's old home, where we were now living, and waiting to hear back from the publisher with whom I had recently spoken about my manuscript. I remembered the sermon we heard at our recent visit to Holy Trinity Church, with the stadium full of saints cheering us on. And for the first time in a long time, I felt as though I could not imagine life being any better.

But that's when everything changed.

I had my laptop out on the kitchen counter at the time, with music setting the backdrop for our work, and it was then that I received an email from Amanda. She wrote to tell me that she had heard back from the publisher and that she was forwarding me their note.

> So, unfortunately, we're not going to pursue publica-
> tion on this one right now. I'm sorry it has taken us so
> long to come to this conclusion, it really was because
> we liked the writing and the idea that we kept trying

to push it. But, please know that we really like Ryan as a person and a potential author. I'm very interested to see where he lands after Oxford. If he ends up in the pastorate, or more academia, or parachurch ministry, or vocational ministry, etc. . . . each of those will have very large ramifications on how this book would reach the market.

Please keep me up to date on Ryan's post-Oxford plans and any other writing he plans on doing. I'd be very happy to revisit this in six months or a year.

"What is it?" Jen asked, looking at me over the top of my laptop screen. "What's wrong?"

Try as I might, I couldn't find any words. So I turned my screen around to let her read it for herself.

"Oh, hon," she said with a sigh. "I am so sorry."

Jen wiped her hands on a hand towel before embracing me in a hug. She told me not to let this get me down. She told me she was sure the book was going to be published, and that this publisher just wasn't the right fit.

I thanked her. Then I told her I was going to get some fresh air.

She nodded, looking me in the face with squinted eyes and a lowered brow, as though she were checking my temperature.

I grabbed my coat and hat from the coatrack and made my way outside. It was now ten o'clock, and I could see the swirl of frosted breath as it left my mouth and rose skyward.

Without thinking where I was going, I walked up the hill behind Lewis's house, toward the pond behind the Kilns. I took a seat on the old brick bench where Lewis used to sit and think and smoke his pipe.

My mind was a blur, spinning from one thought to the next. I thought about what Walter told me several months earlier, about how Lewis struggled with his writing for years. How he used to live in this house and write, long before most folks were familiar with his writing. I thought about how sure I was that things were going to go through this time, and how I really had no idea what this meant for my calling. Prior to this news, I felt so confident in how well everything was lining up. I was sure my book was going to be picked up, and that I would wrap up my studies at Oxford and go on to be a writer. But now, now those plans all seemed to be crumbling in my hands and falling like sand between my fingers.

Not knowing quite what to do, I prayed. And it was in the midst of prayer that the tears began to fall, warming my cheeks in the cold night air.

Is this not what you want for me? I asked, silently. *Is this all just my own dream, and not your plans?*

The night was quiet, with not even the sound of wind blowing a response through the skeletal branches overhead. The still silence of the night seemed to echo the divine silence to my prayers.

But before I got up from the bench, something happened. I say "happened," but if someone was there, they would not have noticed anything happening. Not in the way someone notices a boy riding his bicycle across a street. Or a bird flapping its wings. Though I was sure something had in fact happened then and there.

From my seat on the old brick bench, a feeling of peace washed over me, as though someone had set a warm blanket over my freezing shoulders. It was as though I could feel an arm on my shoulder, and then, words in my ear. Soft, so they weren't quite audible, but clear enough that I was sure they were there.

St. Thérèse of Lisieux once wrote that there are some experiences in life so delicate that we dare not let them out into the air by putting them into words for fear they might be lost or destroyed. There is something of that in this experience.

Then as now, I was sure I felt the Lord's voice as I sat there in the still of the night. I call it the Lord's voice because I am quite sure it was not merely my own thoughts I heard, and because there was no one else there with me. They were words of peace and comfort when all I felt at the time was dread and failure and hopelessness.

I felt as though the Lord was reminding me in that moment that he had plans for this, for all of this, even when I could not see them. It was as though he was right there, incarnate enough to be sitting beside me with an arm around my shoulder, even as my tears fell, encouraging me to dry my eyes, and to rest assured that things were going to work out.

I felt him asking me to trust him.

I stood to leave, but before I had taken a step I noticed something had fallen out of my Bible, which had been sitting open on my lap. It was the French gospel tract I had stumbled upon beneath the Eiffel Tower in Paris the previous spring, the last time I faced a closed door on my writing.

Stooping to pick up the tract, my laughter crackled in the otherwise still night air. I placed the piece of paper back in my Bible, wiped my eyes, and made my way back down the hill to the Kilns, where I found Jen waiting for me in our room. I greeted her with a smile, and she welcomed me with a hug. I pressed my lips to her forehead and rested my cheek on the top of her head. As distraught as I was when I had left, she could notice the peace that had set in somewhere between my leaving and my returning.

C. S. Lewis once wrote an essay on the question of prayer and, specifically, he wrote about those requests of ours that go ungranted. Reflecting on his own prayer life, Lewis wrote that he would quite often find himself gladdened by the thought that specific prayers he made in the past were not granted.

That's the kind of thing people can say only with many years behind them, with countless closed doors, and with years of living in the wake of those closed doors.

My time beside the pond left me in a state of peace at the thought that even if my writing was not to be picked up now, God was working all of this out, and this news did not necessarily mean the door would always remain closed. But that peace did not last long.

With the door on my writing seemingly slammed closed, I turned to my academic work, thinking perhaps this was the path for me at the moment. So I applied to Oxford's master's in Theology program, which I would begin after completing the BA degree—my second—feeling confident this is where we'd be the following year.

As confident as I had been in getting an offer on my manuscript after my call with the publisher back in the States, I was even more confident that my application to Oxford's master's program would be accepted. I realize how ridiculous that sounds. But here's the thing: the Director of Undergraduate Affairs in Oxford's Theology Faculty had written my letter of recommendation. His name was Philip, and I had taken his tutorial in modern theology that year. He said he would be happy to recommend me for the master's program.

Philip wore glasses and was often dressed in a cardigan and checkered shirt. His office was in an airy third-floor space that looked out over the city's rooftops. Philip described prophets as "socially transforming," which made me pause long enough from my frantic note-taking to lift my head.

"Well they are, aren't they?" he asked.

"Prophets care about justice." His voice grew in excitement and seriousness. "They care about their message, and they're not afraid to stand up to those in authority to get it across. They want to change the world!"

Philip quoted ancient and modern theologians verbatim during our time together, applying their words to contemporary issues, and making it all seem so practical. He asked difficult questions and smiled graciously at my response, even when we didn't agree. He never made me feel bad for what I didn't know, but instead would drop hints at authors I might read to brush up where needed. And he made me feel good about what I *did* know. He was my favorite tutor.

"You have a theologian's mind," he told me once, with a slight smile. That was the best compliment I'd ever received in a tutorial.

Pair Philip's recommendation with strong marks in my other tutorials, and positive feedback from my other tutors, and I assumed I was a shoo-in. Not because I was so smart—I was still deathly self-conscious of how much smarter than me everyone else at Oxford seemed to be—but because I had done what I needed to do. I was so confident in this going through, in fact, that I didn't even apply anywhere else. I loved Oxford, we had a rich community of friends, and Jen I were both feeling much better about our being there after moving to the Kilns. We both figured this was where we would be. We were wrong.

> We are sorry to inform you that you have not been
> offered a spot . . .

That was all I could read of the graduate committee's letter before looking away.

With the doors closed not only on my writing, but now also on my academic career, it felt as though the ground had fallen out from beneath my feet. I was left standing there in midair, like one of those cartoon characters, with a stupid look on my face, bracing for the thud that was sure to follow. We returned to the States again that winter to spend the holidays with our family. I had no idea what to do next.

10

Experience

A Lamppost in the Snow

"Why are you trying so hard?" a bald, spectacled man asked a sea of eyes from his spot at the front of Oxford's town hall.

His question was the most embarrassingly obvious question I had heard in a long time. It was as though he had walked into a room full of naked people all pretending they were dressed up in beautiful gowns and brilliant suits and said, "Hey, you're all naked. . . . What's with that?"

"You've gotten into Oxford, and still, you're working so hard to show others, 'I am not a bum,'" he continued. "We all know something is wrong, and we want to prove we're all right."

The man was a pastor from New York City by the name of Tim Keller. He was in Oxford giving a series of lectures to students.

Some have suggested Tim Keller is the next C. S. Lewis, which always makes me cringe. I'm told it makes Keller cringe, too. My skin begins to crawl whenever I hear someone is "the next C. S. Lewis," as though we need *another* C. S. Lewis. As if the church is somehow like the NBA, desperately searching for another Michael Jordan. The church still has Lewis's words. For those who might find them helpful, they're easy enough to get your hands on. For those who find his books less than helpful, perhaps a bit dry or dense or "old-fashioned," God will give new teachers, and new voices.

Of course, Keller does not shy away from admitting Lewis's influence on his own work. I've heard him say you can tell how much time he spent on his sermon by how frequently he quotes C. S. Lewis. When he's short on time, he defaults to Lewis.

Knowing his appreciation for Lewis's work, I wrote Keller's assistant to introduce myself and to extend an invite for Tim and his wife, Kathy, to join me at the Kilns for tea while they were in town. Since he was scheduled to give more than a half dozen lectures in a week, I wasn't holding my breath. Which is why I was pleasantly surprised to receive a reply saying they'd love to take me up on the offer.

Busy as I was reading and writing essays, I managed to sneak away from the library to the old, cavernous town-hall building in the middle of the city center for a couple of Keller's talks that week. And when I did, I found myself looking forward to our time together.

"Mary . . ." Pastor Keller said at the close of his lectures in a hushed voice, reflecting on the scene of Mary's encounter with the resurrected Jesus in the garden. It is, perhaps, one of the most vivid scenes of despair in the entire Bible.

Upon finding the tomb empty, Mary begs this stranger— who she thinks is the garden owner—to tell her where he's put

Jesus' body. You can hear the desperation in her voice and see the tears in her swollen eyes. She hasn't slept in days, hasn't eaten. She's hurting and confused, and she cannot see that the One she is searching for is the One now staring her in the face.

That is, of course, until Jesus speaks. Of all things to say at such a moment, Jesus simply calls her by name.

"Mary . . ." Pastor Keller repeated, in the same hushed voice. After a pause, Keller spoke up again. "You will find you do not know who you are until he calls you by name. He will show you what you're made for."

Snowflakes were falling over the city center when I hopped on my bike late one night after Tim Keller's lectures. The city was blanketed in a good two inches of light, fluffy snow as my bike tires crept through the roads. I was doing my best not to end up sprawled out in a pile of clothes on top of my bike in the now-white High Street.

The city was particularly quiet. It was as though the snow had somehow muffled the usual noise of students and buses and cabs, leaving only still air in its wake.

I turned off High Street at University Church of the Virgin St. Mary and passed slowly by the massive stone dome of the Radcliffe Camera. To my amazement, I was the only one around. Not a single other soul was there. No one walking. No one cycling. Just me.

The snow was still falling, but only barely. It had already covered the street and the surrounding colleges. The sight of the Bridge of Sighs all dressed in white, lit up by the nearby lamppost, took my breath away.

I took a cautious foot off my bike pedal and stood there, straddling my bike, staring at this lamppost in the snow. It was radiating light, illuminating the arched, stone bridge and stained-glass windows. I found myself thinking what a gift this was.

I wondered if it was not on a similar night, many years before, that Lewis found himself in the middle of the Oxford city center, after the snow had fallen, with his breath taken away by a lone lamppost standing in a white field of snow. I wondered if a sight like this had long ago captivated Lewis's imagination and inspired his pen.

When the snow began to fall over the wood at the foot of Shotover Hill, just behind the Kilns, Debbie liked to point out the view of the forest Lewis would have enjoyed.

"His desk sat right here," she'd say, motioning with both hands to the center of the second-floor room where he used to write, just in front of the window looking out toward Shotover Hill. "And if you have ever walked through Shotover Forest in the snow, I mean, that's Narnia!"

After about a year of giving tours at the Kilns, it became almost second nature. But I still enjoyed it. I liked meeting the new people who would come through. I still loved sharing stories about C. S. Lewis. Most of all, I relished the opportunity to introduce Lewis to folks who didn't know much about his work.

As familiar and routine as it had become, there were still some surprises. A few will likely always stand out in my mind.

One Saturday afternoon, I gave a tour to a group of Korean exchange students from London. About halfway through the tour, while I was pointing out a photo in the dining room and telling a story, one of the students gave me a puzzled look.

I had been talking about a point toward the end of C. S. Lewis's life, when his wife, Joy, was struck with bone cancer. I told them how this cancer had begun to consume her body from the inside out. She was not only hospitalized, her medical staff did not think she would leave the hospital alive.

But then, something curious happened. Rather miraculously, Joy's cancer went into a period of remission, and her bones soon began to grow strong and whole again. Her medical staff was stunned. She was later allowed to leave the hospital and move into the Kilns with Lewis and her two boys: David, the older, and Douglas Gresham, the younger of the two.

At this point in the tour, I pointed out a picture hanging on the wall in the dining room. It was a black-and-white photo of Lewis standing beside his bride, Joy, leaning against the waist-high stone wall in the garden in front of the Kilns. The happy couple, now reunited, enjoying their married life together at the Kilns after being married on what was thought to be Joy's deathbed.

In some ways, it was a photo of Lewis not so unlike others. He was wearing the same baggy trousers and ill-fitting jacket his father used to give him a hard time about, as though he picked them off the rack without bothering about his size. In other ways, it was a rare photo of Lewis. He had heavy bags under his eyes, and there was little joy to be found in his face, even with his Joy returned to him in renewed health. And that was the curious thing about the photo: if anyone should be looking unwell, it was Joy. And yet, there she was, looking as though she was enjoying life as usual, holding a cane in one hand, sure, but healthy-faced and petting a shaggy dog with her other hand. With a half-smile, she looked surprisingly well. Proud, even, as though she had just pulled one over on death. Given that she'd been through hell and back, it was surprising that Lewis is the one who looks like hell.

At one point, in a moment of heartbreaking honesty, Lewis asked Joy to visit him were he to ever find himself on his own deathbed, if she was allowed.

"Allowed!" she declared. "Heaven would have a job to hold me; and as for hell, I'd break it into bits."

Lewis recounts this period in his book *A Grief Observed*, which he wrote not long after Joy's death—originally using a pseudonym for the pure fact that he got stark naked in his grief and walked around in it. In a letter to a friend around this time, Lewis tells the curious story of how, shortly after Joy's cancer went into a state of remission, and her bones began to grow strong, his own bones grew weak and brittle. She was soon up and walking about again, while Lewis was faced with the onset of osteoporosis.

In this letter, Lewis mentions his friend Charles Williams's idea of substitution. Williams thought that if we pray to God for our loved ones, asking God to have mercy and bring healing to their body, God may very well choose to answer our prayers by giving them our good health, and, in their place, allow us to carry their burden in our own body. While Lewis never claimed to believe this is what had actually happened to him, he did mention the idea.

The photo in the Kilns dining room was taken at the time of their little switcheroo. Call it funny timing, but Williams may have called it an answer to prayer. Just not in the way we tend to think of it.

"It seems like he had some superstitious ideas," this Korean student with the puzzled face said to me at this point in the tour. "Maybe even unbiblical."

I smiled at the student's comment, telling him I appreciated his honesty. I clarified that this wasn't actually Lewis's idea, and he never said that this was what he believed had happened, though the timing of it all was quite stunning, and the photo taken at the time does a great job of telling the story.

But I used this student's comment to make a point.

"Personally, I appreciate any story that shows how Lewis might have been a bit unconventional. I think a lot of people try to make Lewis into a saint, or even a cipher for our own opinions and ideas. But he wasn't a saint, and I don't think he fits neatly into the mold we've made for him.

"He was, of course, a very bright guy who was trying to live out his Christian faith, and he used what he had to help others do the same. Perhaps that's as much as any of us can hope for."

The student nodded and feigned a smile, but it was clear he was less than content with my response.

Another tour I will always remember—I might even call it my favorite— wasn't even supposed to be my tour. Not initially. A middle-aged couple wrote Debbie to ask about getting a tour of the Kilns with their teenage son, which was nothing out of the ordinary. The catch was their son had cerebral palsy and was in a wheelchair. They wrote to make sure it wouldn't be any trouble to get around the house. Not knowing whether or not they might need an extra hand, Debbie asked me to join her for the tour.

The couple showed up at the Kilns pushing their teenage son, Kirk, to the front door along the gravel footpath. I can only imagine what it must have been like traveling all the way to

England from Texas with a teenage son in a wheelchair, but they arrived looking as though they had just won the lottery. I was even more surprised when they told me they had just finished visiting family in Scotland. Clearly, they were not about to let some narrow hallways and the tight corners of an old house get in their way.

Though they must have been in their fifties—hints of brown stuck out from her otherwise gray hair and his had given itself completely to the gray—they both brimmed with energy. They came to the home to celebrate their son's fifteenth birthday.

"Kirk is one of C. S. Lewis's biggest fans," his mom told me from the front of the house.

Kirk had been straight-faced up to this point, but at that comment, he flashed an electric grin.

During my year and a half or so of giving tours at the Kilns, I met loads of people who traveled thousands of miles, from all corners of the globe, to see C. S. Lewis's old home. To see where he used to live and write. To see the world that inspired his words. Some knew quite a bit about Lewis's life and his work. Others knew nothing much about him at all; they came because an excited friend had dragged them along. But this was the first time I had met anyone who had sacrificed so much to get there. And who seemed so happy to do so. Of course, great sacrifices can feel like winning the lottery if it means showing someone how deeply we love them.

I told Kirk I knew the feeling.

164

I was still thinking about the lamppost in the snow and writing and inspiration when I had Tim and Kathy Keller to the Kilns for a tour and tea at the end of that week.

I knew Tim was a fan of Lewis's writing. What I didn't realize was how intimately Kathy knew and appreciated his work.

Their cab pulled up to the Kilns on a Friday afternoon and I greeted them at the front door. Seeing Pastor Keller up close, I was surprised by how tall he was, which only made me more nervous.

Both of them had been to the Kilns before, they told me. I learned that Kathy had actually visited the house shortly after Lewis passed away. His brother, Warnie, had shown her around. She told me about how, as a young girl, she had written Lewis, and that he had responded to her letters.

Tim pulled the book *Letters to Children* off the bookshelf in the front room, thumbed his way to the back pages, and showed me Kathy's letter.

30 November 1962

Dear Kathy,

Thanks for your very kind letter and greetings. I was 64 yesterday. I am so glad you like my books. With all good wishes.

Yours sincerely,

C. S. Lewis

Kathy gazed out the front window at the garden and walked from photo to photo, looking closely at the faces in the frames. I told them about Lewis's life in the house, the story of Joy moving in, and the end of their stories. Tim sat in a recliner in a corner of the front room, listening with a hint of a smile. They took turns asking questions, most of which I was able to answer. I was surprised to notice neither one of them, in our two hours together, checked their phone or otherwise seemed to have their mind elsewhere. They were completely present and personable.

After showing Tim and Kathy around the home, and sharing all the stories I knew—many of which, I was relieved to hear, they had not heard before—we gathered in the dining room for a full English tea, which Debbie had prepared before leaving to run errands.

Even though we had never met before, talking with them there that afternoon felt as familiar as talking with my pastor and his wife from back home. I was still passing around the scones and tea when Tim asked me what I was hoping to do after Oxford. I confessed that I was hoping to be a writer, though there had not been much luck with it lately.

They both cringed.

"Writing comes from experience," Tim told me from his seat across the table, explaining his reservations about young people who want to write.

"It's important to serve others, and to have the experience of doing funerals and weddings. To be with someone when they pass away," Tim said. "That kind of experience inspires our writing."

I nodded, my heart sinking a bit.

We finished our tea and I thanked them both for coming. I told them how much I appreciated meeting them, and how I wished Jen could have been there.

"Maybe next time," Tim told me with a smile, handing me a copy of his book *The Reason for God*, in which he had scribbled a signature and a note.

I said good-bye to Tim and Kathy as they climbed into their cab.

"Writing comes from experience," I said, repeating Tim's words as I turned and made my way back inside.

Douglas Gresham was seated on a couch, leaning over a newspaper spread out over a coffee table in the lobby of a High Street hotel the first time I met him. It's the kind of hotel where politicians and movie stars stay when they visit the city. Not the kind of hotel students often set foot in. At least, not students like me.

Though I had seen pictures of Douglas before, and knew what he looked like, it was the knee-high riding boots that gave him away. His trademark look, I suppose.

Douglas wore a finely kept salt-and-pepper beard, paired with a white turtleneck sweater and off-white moleskin pants, tucked into his tall, black boots. Over his sweater hung a long-chained silver cross.

"It's a gift from my daughter," he told me later in conversation.

I had written Douglas, the younger of C. S. Lewis's two step-sons—though he was now old enough to have nearly a dozen grandchildren—to ask if he might be visiting Oxford in the near future, and to see if he might be willing to address the Society. Knowing Douglas lived nearly two thousand miles away, I figured it was a long shot. Once again, I was happily surprised to find a note in my inbox saying he'd be pleased to come for a visit.

Douglas spoke in short, pointed sentences as we walked from his hotel to the college where he'd be speaking that night. His accent was a strange combination of British and Australian, as he had lived in Australia for many years after leaving England.

Called

"How would you like me to introduce you?" I asked Douglas from our spot in the hallway outside a packed room that evening. "How about as a successful cattle farmer?" Douglas replied with a half-smile. He was joking, but only half joking. Knowing he became a cattle farmer when he lived in Australia, I went ahead and introduced him that way. The introduction was met with a round of laughter and applause. Douglas grinned.

Douglas spoke openly and honestly about his childhood at the Kilns with C. S. Lewis and Joy, about the peaks and the valleys of life in Oxford. He shared about the time he prayed to God from Holy Trinity Church that his mother's cancer might be healed. He told us the ache and loneliness he felt when he said good-bye at such a young age not only to his mother, but also to his birth father and stepfather within just a few years.

"Everyone close to me was now gone," he said, with pained eyes.

After talking for nearly an hour, Douglas took questions for another full hour. When he had signed a couple dozen autographs and smiled for photos in one of the cloisters of St. John's College, I walked Douglas back to his hotel. I thanked him for his generosity, for making the trip to Oxford to be with us, and for sharing such deeply personal stories. I told him I admired his honesty, which I told him I appreciated personally.

"Not everyone is so willing to share such painful experiences."

"No," he said with a pause, "but perhaps more should be."

Turning my head, I saw the look of pain now returned to Douglas's face. Though, of course, it bore the marks of a few more years, it was still the same face of the young boy who was, for a time, privileged to enjoy incredible conversations and laughter and life with his mother and stepfather at the Kilns.

Maybe Douglas was right. Perhaps more of us should be honest with our painful stories. Maybe it would make us feel less alone. To place our palms with fingers outstretched against the windowpane of this confusing, complex life that separates as well as unites us, and to hold them there, so others might approach and place their hands against the glass separating us and be reminded that it is okay, that we are human, and we are alive.

With memories of Hayley's now-distant smile and the pain of closed doors from publishers and Tim Keller's words about writing coming from experience all swirling around in my mind, I told Douglas I agreed.

11

Wilderness, II

New Life

Oxford's exam system is about as dreadful as you'd imagine. Since there are no official grades along the way, the entire degree comes down to how you do on your final, cumulative exams. Mine would amount to seven three-hour, handwritten exams spread across just six days at the end of my two years of study.

Most students spent much less time preparing for exams than I did. Most Oxford students also had better, sharper tools with which to work. I would read other students' work and feel as though I was writing my essays in crayon. It takes a while to get very far writing in crayon.

When it came time to begin preparing for finals—"revisions," as these preparations are called—I was typically the first to sit down and get to the day's work when the Harris Manchester library doors opened at eight thirty in the morning. It was not uncommon to find a handful of other students still in the Harris

Manchester library with me when it closed for the night at eleven o'clock sharp. Folks at the Kilns were usually in bed or on their way there when I got home in the evenings, where I'd pick it up again until I fell asleep, usually around three in the morning. Then I'd wake up around seven or seven thirty and be out of the house, before others were up, to do it all over again. This was my routine, six days a week, for about three months. I worked half days on Sunday.

One morning I was biking to college, past the shops in Headington and down Headington Hill, when I had the strangest feeling. It was as though I was recalling a dream, but it was stronger than simply a memory. I could feel it in my body, the feeling of grabbing an electric fence as a young boy playing in the farm fields. I could feel its surge even as I rode past the market and the fish-and-chips shop and Emma Watson's old school on my way to college.

In high school, I worked at a summer camp for folks with disabilities for three summers. Short of working as a tour guide at the Kilns, this was my all-time favorite job. It was there I met the only saints I've ever known. But something happened one morning that still haunts me at times. In the middle of laughing and joking around, in an instant I watched as a camper in his forties fell on the floor, bare-chested, his body convulsing and his eyes rolled back in his head. I stood there in shock for several seconds, not knowing what to do, before rushing off to get the nurse. After a few minutes of helping him sit up in bed so the nurse could check him out, we started our day as if nothing had happened. Apparently it was not his first seizure.

After a quick search online, I read that a lack of sleep is a potential cause of seizures. I had never had a seizure before, and the idea that I might have had one just before getting out of bed that morning scared me. Suddenly, more than ever, I found myself wishing Jen were there. Not only so that I wouldn't kill myself with my study schedule. And not only because I missed her since returning to Oxford on my own after celebrating Christmas and New Year's with our family back in the States once again. But so that she'd be able to tell me whether this seizure was all just some terrible dream.

Saturday was when I did my grocery shopping for the week, after reading through past essays, outlining practice responses, and making flow charts with names and dates of old, dead white men. I usually shopped in Headington, and then rode back to the Kilns with plastic grocery bags overflowing from the metal Tesco hand basket zip-tied to the bike frame behind my seat, with several additional bags dangling off each side of my handlebars.

One Saturday during this period, I remember walking through the aisles, wondering what I had come there for, and trying to figure out whether this was real or if I was dreaming. I eventually filled a basket with the things I could remember usually getting—tortillas, bread, eggs, soy milk, crunchy peanut butter, pesto sauce, the cheapest meat I could find, pasta, and some fruits and vegetables. I made my way out of the market and back to the Kilns, still unsure whether or not I was awake.

There were times that spring when I wondered if I'd ever get home, both to the place called home as well as to the home inside myself.

Called

During our time living at the Kilns, a red-framed photograph of Jen and me sat on the mantle of the brick fireplace in Warnie's old bedroom. She was smiling widely in the photo, as was I, and her head was resting on my shoulder. The frame was a gift, and italic silver letters were scrawled across it that read, "Smile."

Months after moving in, this red-framed photo had become a fixture of the room; I hardly noticed it. But one day, as I was leaving the house, this photo caught my eye and I stopped. Looking at Jen's smile with her head on my shoulder, I realized how very much I wanted my best friend to be there with me. To see. To hold. To talk. It had been months since I had last seen her.

Returning after Christmas for our second year in Oxford on my own, life in Oxford felt so empty without Jen there. I found myself missing having that someone to talk with, to share life with, and to be honest with. The thing is, when you're married, you can say things to your spouse you can't say to anyone else. Things you're thinking. The kind of things that, if you were to share with anyone else, they'd think you were evil. But you can share them with your spouse, because they know you're evil. They live with you.

I found myself trying to remember how Jen smells when I hug her. I found myself missing the way she smiled when she was reading, when she thought no one was watching. The way she tucked her hair behind her ear, and how she folded her hands in front of her when she talked. The way she said a hundred words with just a smile. Or a half-smile. She's efficient, Jen.

Jen isn't about excess, in anything. She's sincere and considerate, but she never layers it on. She knows when I need a compliment, and she gives it. But most times, she only tells me what I need. And I think that's probably the way it ought to be.

I found myself missing the feeling of her head resting on my chest when I lie in bed at night, and the sound of her soft breathing when she has fallen asleep before me. I found myself missing her eyes—eyes that speak more truth than a hundred words.

One of the first things God said about Adam, when he was still busy naming all the animals from sunup to sundown, was that it wasn't good for him to be alone.

I was returning to the Kilns late one evening after a long day at Harris Manchester when I found myself standing in the middle of the tall, naked birch trees with their white bark, reaching their long, spindly arms high up into the air, as if to point out the stars in the pale night sky. And it reminded me of my late evening walks back to the Kilns with Jen after a night out in the city center. It reminded me of when I pointed out the stars to Jen and asked her if she found it mind-blowing that we could look up in the sky and see the same constellations from six thousand miles away, back home in Washington State.

That night, I scratched a note to Jen from the desk in our room with a line from a poem by the Victorian poet, Elizabeth Barrett Browning:

Gaze up at the stars knowing that I see the same sky
and wish the same sweet dreams.

It was here late one evening, from my desk in Warnie's old room, that I found myself staring at Jen's photo on my computer wallpaper in the early morning hours, after putting in another full day at the college library. The photo was taken at the Gorge Amphitheatre, back home in Washington, at a concert we had enjoyed together shortly after we began dating. Her eyes were staring back into mine, and for a moment, it felt like she was really there, staring right back at me.

Even though I was alone, in our study, and Jen was some six thousand miles away, in my mind I heard her ask, "What? What is it?" And so, in my mind, without thinking twice, I told this photo of Jen from nearly a decade before that I missed her. I told her I missed her so much.

She asked me why, and I told her because I was in England, going back to school, and she was still in the States. She looked surprised, sitting on this bluff overlooking the Columbia River, as though she were trying to wrap her mind around it all. After a moment, she asked if I was enjoying it, if I was happy. And I told her I was. I told her I really did like it here, but it's just that I missed her when we're apart. She told me she understood. And, in my mind, she said she was sure she missed me, too, and that she was certain she'd be there with me if she could.

And so that's when I told her the reason she was still back in Washington State, and we were now six thousand miles apart. I told her how we had traveled home to be with our family for Christmas during the second year of my studies in Oxford, and that's when we found out that she was pregnant with our first child. Her eyes grew big.

"Reeeally?" she said, drawing out the word. "I am?" I smiled. And told her yes, she was.

She asked how long we'd been married at this point.

"Five and a half years."

"You mean I have to wait that long to get pregnant?!" she asked with a playful smile, revealing just how excited she was.

I told her she was still back at home because she had been terribly sick. That she was feeling nauseous all the time, and that she had lost some twenty pounds in just a few weeks. I explained that she didn't feel up to flying that far on her own yet.

I told her that Leann, her sister, was really sick during her pregnancy the year before, and so we had figured she would be, too.

"You mean Leann has a baby before me?! What about Hayley? Do I have a baby before Hayley?"

I paused for a moment, before assuring her she did.

"What?" she asked, her brow lowered and her eyebrows scrunched together. "Why'd you pause?"

"Oh, nothing. I . . . I was just thinking how much I know you wanted to be the first. I'm sorry."

"It's okay," she told me with a smile, and her hair brushed across her face as the summer breeze played with it. She was still beaming at this news, with her eyes glimmering in the afternoon sun as she stared back into mine.

And then, that was it. That was the end of our conversation, as I realized I was still seated at my desk, staring at my computer screen, having an imaginary conversation with the wife of my youth.

The photo of our child's ultrasound scan taken while Jen and I were both home for Christmas stood on the corner of my desk, with the words "A Gift from God," sketched on the frame. A reminder of the reality of the new life that we would soon be welcoming into the world. Together. I smiled in the darkness of my silent room, even as I felt more alone than when this imaginary conversation began. I washed my face in the cold water of the bathroom sink, pressed a white hand towel to my forehead, and then returned to my books.

The worst part about being alone for months on end is the thoughts that run around and around in my head. To be fair, I spend most days living inside my head—hoping that when I finally open my mouth or put pen to paper, what comes out will matter. But being alone for long stretches felt like I was constantly bumping into the walls of my own mind with no hope of ever finding my way out. And the longer I lived like this, the harder it was to actually interact with others, even while I was longing for a voice from the outside to break up the endless cycle of my own threadbare thoughts. For me, that was the worst part about loneliness: chasing my own mental tail without getting anywhere.

This struggle with loneliness and the limits of my own mind reminded me of something Lewis wrote years ago, on the value of reading other authors:

> In reading great literature I become a thousand men and yet remain myself. . . . I see with a myriad of eyes, but it is still I who see. (*An Experiment in Criticism* 141).

I am not completely sure this was what Lewis had in mind when he wrote these words—nor am I so sure it matters—but it was in the midst of these exhausting mental laps that I began to feel as though I knew, perhaps for the first time, what his words meant.

Fatigue and loneliness weren't the only battles I was fighting. I was also dealing with an overwhelming amount of stress about my approaching exams. The kind of stress that tears up your insides. And I wasn't alone.

A friend at college told me about a girl at another college a couple years earlier who had done well enough during her time at Oxford to earn herself a full scholarship to Harvard. Unfortunately, the pressure of her looming final exams grew week by week until, finally, it was all too much for her. Before she even had a chance to take her exams, with her spot at Harvard waiting for her regardless of how she actually did on them, someone found her body hanging in her room.

Another friend told me that the city doesn't allow students to go up the tower of University Church of the Virgin St. Mary—the tallest point in Oxford's city center—in the weeks leading up to exams. To prevent jumpers.

Pitting some of the most driven students in the world against what is quite possibly one of the most rigorous exam systems seems like a terrible idea. Cambridge students recently voted to change their own exams from a cumulative schedule, like Oxford, to a more typical, end-of-the-semester exam system. But this was Oxford. Little had changed in the past nine hundred years.

Maybe they were nothing more than myths, the story of the girl, as well as the one about the tower. Nothing more than legends students tell one another to build up the drama and tension of it all. But seeing the nervous looks on the faces of finalists around town—"finalists" is what Oxford calls its undergrads in their final year—I thought the stories might very well be true. Seeing the look on my own gaunt face in the mirror before bed at night, and when I awoke in the morning, I was pretty sure they were not simply legends.

Riding to the Kilns late one evening after another full day of studies at college, I was surprised when I passed the palm tree at the bottom of Kilns Lane to see how tired it looked. The winter had not treated it well. Its giant palm fronds were now droopy

Called

and dry and brittle, as if they might fall off at the hint of a breeze. Struggling to make my way up the final stretch of road leading back to the Kilns that night, I wondered whether the tree would make it through the winter.

Once, when I was an undergrad at Western Washington University and feeling particularly stressed and tired by all the work I was pouring into finals, my mom sent me a letter. On a piece of Winnie the Pooh stationery, she told me she would rather I be happy than get good grades. I have kept that note tucked away in my journal to this day.

My mom called from time to time while I was revising for exams in Oxford. She'd Skype me from my desk in the library, so I could hear her on my headphones, then I'd type my response. She'd tell me about how her patients would say to her that she must be so proud to have a son studying at Oxford, and that she'd reply that she was, but that she was more proud of my heart. One time she called and said she didn't want to bug me, but that there was something she had wanted to tell me for a while. She told me she was sure that if C. S. Lewis were alive and knew what I was doing, he would be proud.

I could not type a response.

I took a break from studies late one Sunday afternoon to grab a quick bite before returning to the library. Making my way to the sandwich shop down the lane from Harris Manchester, I passed by a man sitting on the sidewalk with his back against the stone

180

building and a blanket over his arched legs. Almost as soon as he could ask if I had any change to spare, I cut him off.

"I'm sorry."

He apologized for bothering me, and I told him it was no bother at all, as I continued my way to the sandwich shop. Immediately, my mind darted to the change in my pocket. The change I could easily have given him. I thought about the many ways in which I'd been helped out along the way, the sort of help that had allowed me to even be passing by the man at this moment.

These thoughts continued to play on a loop as I ordered my sandwich. I left the shop a few minutes later, sandwich in hand. Guilt ridden, I decided to cross the street instead of passing back by this man a second time, now carrying my food.

As I crossed the street, without any effort on my part, I remembered the old story of the so-called Good Samaritan, and the "religious" ones who passed by on the opposite side of the street. As I walked, head hanging low, I realized this familiar story wasn't about those religious people way back when. It was about me.

That's when I felt pressed to turn around and offer this man my sandwich. A battle raged inside of me as I walked, with one voice encouraging me to turn around and offer to help this man I had just snubbed, and another voice telling me it would be embarrassing to do so. This battle continued to rage inside of me until I finally bit down into the crunchy bread, sealing my decision. At that moment, I realized I didn't actually understand Christianity.

Walking back to Harris Manchester, the thought of returning to revisions for exams and studying theology while completely misunderstanding Christianity was enough to make me sick. I could not finish my sandwich.

For Oxford undergrads, Friday nights meant drinking. And lots of it. Every college has its own bar where students can find cheap drinks, loud music, and a chance to throw off the past week's reading and essays and sleepless nights. When the college bar shuts down, there are plenty of pubs around town to visit for more drinks and good times. Of course, when the pubs shut down, that's when it's time to move on to the clubs, which stay open until the break of dawn, when people finally wander home through the city like zombies dressed in gowns and tuxedos.

One evening that spring, I found myself particularly tired and lonely, standing awkwardly in the middle of a club dance floor at three in the morning, with music I could feel in my chest as much as I could hear in my ears. Friends from college were dancing and hanging on one another, and I wondered what I was doing there. I decided to take a bus home until I found my head spinning and my stomach churning. I hit the "Stop" button a half mile or so after it picked me up, just in time to get out and allow the fresh, cool night air to wash over me, like a balm for my head and stomach. I walked the remaining two and a half miles back to the Kilns.

Most Friday nights, my Finnish friends Olli and his wife Salla would have me over to their place for takeout and a movie. They were some of my closest friends in Oxford, though they became more like family than friends.

Olli and Salla both spoke in Finnish accents, which I think made them self-conscious because they often asked me to say the prayer when we ate together. He had a full head of hair when they were first married; she had hair the color of sunshine, which seemed fitting, somehow. Olli was brilliant, though he'd never admit it. I think he had his PhD in theology before he was twenty-five. He was also incredibly blunt and had one of the driest senses of humor, which was probably why we got along so well. Salla had a radiant smile, a sharp mind, and she was one of the sweetest people I'd ever met. Like Jen, you might not know it if you have only just met her, but Salla was also deceptively tough.

That spring, she gave birth to a beautiful baby boy—their second—but not without a delivery that Olli described as looking like something out of a *Kill Bill* film. Things were so bad that she broke her tailbone from pushing. She couldn't sit comfortably for months.

"I just knew that if I didn't get him out of me, he was going to die," Salla told me with wide eyes a few weeks afterward as I held their swaddled son in my arms. Tobias was baptized just before I left Oxford, and they asked me if I would be his godfather. I consider that one of my short life's great honors.

Salla would often turn in after our Friday night movies, and Olli and I would stay up late into the night, talking in their living room about Norse mythology and comic book films and music. And then, when we'd gotten serious enough, we'd talk about what in the world we were supposed to be doing with our lives. Around one or two in the morning, I'd brave the frigid night air and bike the five miles or so back to the Kilns, dodging zombies dressed in tuxedos and gowns in the city center.

On my last night in Oxford, I thanked them both for having me over on Friday nights. I told them that, without realizing it, they might have saved my marriage.

I knew May first was coming long before it actually arrived. I had been tracking it on my calendar like a hunter tracks a bear on the horizon. I dreaded it with everything in me. And by the time the anniversary of Hayley's death finally arrived, I was still unprepared.

Try as I might to focus on the words on the page in front of me that evening in the dimly lit lower reading room of the Bodleian Library, I could not. The rhythmic, paced beep . . . beep . . . beeping sound of books being checked in threw me back to the early morning hours I spent praying beside Hayley's bed in the ICU, with Mat Kearney's voice crooning, "I would take a bullet for you" from the stereo in the windowsill and the sound of the breathing machine beside her bed keeping beat. It made me think of all those things I'd longed to share with her but couldn't: the memorial tattoos we had inked on our wrists the day before her funeral; the playlist I had promised I'd make for her but didn't have time to finish before she was gone; the fact that she was finally an aunt, and would soon be one twice-over.

Beep . . . beep . . . beep.

I grabbed my things, threw them in my bag, and rode home with tears streaking down my cheeks as I scaled Headington Hill.

It was Christmas Eve when we first found out I had been offered a spot at Oxford, and Jen's family was all gathered around the dining room table at her grandparent's house. We were late getting there, and I was barely through the door when Jen was already sharing the news with her family. I'll never forget the look on Hayley's face that evening. While everyone else was celebrating, getting up from their seats to offer a hug and "Congrats,"

Hayley was doing her best to feign a smile. She didn't want us to leave. Of course, none of us knew it at the time, but she would be the first to leave, and we would be left doing our best to feign smiles for years to come.

I didn't realize until I got back to the Kilns late that night that I had dressed in all black early that morning. Black jacket over a black T-shirt, with faded black jeans.

Lying in bed that evening, I watched as pink roses floated on the River Cherwell from one side of the backs of my eyelids to the other. I listened to the sound of the laugh Hayley swore didn't sound like her sister's echoing off the walls. I read again, as if for the first time, the words of the last text message she ever sent me.

Beep . . . beep . . . beep.

My fingers clenched tight into my pillow, and I pressed my face firmly against the wet pillowcase. And suddenly, without any effort on my part, I imagined in place of my pillow, across the head of my bed, a lion. With my fingers still clenching the pillow, I suddenly felt as though I was gripping the lion's fur instead, resting my head on its side, rising and falling slowly, steadily, rhythmically. And in a strange, almost magical way that I feel silly now struggling to explain, my tears stopped and I drifted to sleep.

There were times that spring when I wondered if I'd ever make it home. As much to the place called home as to the home inside myself. And every once in a while, a vivid scene struck me.

It was a scene of a little girl—ten, maybe—with flowing chocolate-brown curls bouncing on her shoulders, running across a pea-gravel playground toward me, wearing a wide, orange-slice grin. She was nearly out of breath with excitement by the time she finally reached me, the crunch-crunch of her footsteps chasing her all the way. She'd stop herself some ten feet before she got to me and, still wearing that grin, call out, "Come chase me, Daddy. Chase me to the end of the earth and push me on the swing that looks out where the sun goes to bed each night, where the moon rises to keep watch." And then she'd turn and take off like a shot, just like that.

When I found myself worried about whether or not I'd ever make it home—usually in the early morning hours, sitting at my desk in the dark, missing my wife and wondering what I was doing—I would promise myself that I'd one day chase that little girl to the end of the earth.

One of my favorite theologians has said one reason we need stories is because they remind us who we are. They remind us of the character of the person we're trying to be, and of the community of which we're a part. Without stories, he said, we forget who we are. The novelist and memoirist Frederick Buechner once wrote that to lose track of our stories is to be deeply impoverished. It is to be bankrupt. And sometimes we do; we lose track of our stories and forget who we are, and we need others to remind us. Sometimes we need those who know us most closely to remind us how to find our way home.

I was mostly lost that spring, in a whirlwind of loneliness and exhaustion and anxiety, when I received an unexpected note from home. It was from Jen's cousin, a red-haired high school senior who was preparing to graduate, and who had been working on college applications earlier in the year. He wrote to pass along an essay he had written for one of his applications. The prompt had asked him to write about someone who had somehow shaped him into the person he was today.

To my surprise, he had written about me. *Me?* I asked silently as I read his note. *Surely this is a mistake.*

His essay was short, maybe a couple pages. Basically a string of short anecdotes. He wrote about the time we first met, at one of Jen's family get-togethers, when my wife's large extended family crammed into her grandparents' house for birthday cake and small talk and cold ham on dinner rolls. He wrote about the time I took him off guard by shaking his small hand, asking how he was doing and what his teachers were like. He was nine years old that Sunday afternoon we first met, and he said he walked away scratching his head, not knowing what to do with being asked such things by his oldest cousin's new boyfriend.

He wrote about the time we delivered more than one hundred dollars worth of pens and pencils and notebooks to a school's office after reading a story in our local newspaper about its supplies being stolen just before Christmas. He wrote about the time he stood in the back of the church, with his tie and white shirt and pleated slacks, and watched as I talked and prayed with folks who knew Hayley, mostly high school kids, for several hours. He wrote about how my life had helped him see the importance of putting others first, and how, when his dad lost his job and his parents needed him to help out more, he decided against turning out for a sport that final spring of his high school career so he could be home more to lend a hand with car rides for his younger brothers and sisters, and to help around the house.

In a not-so-small way, I was devastated by this note. Seated there at my desk on the second floor of the Harris Manchester library, his letter grabbed me by the shoulders and shook me awake. I was overwhelmed by gratitude, mostly, but also by a sense of how very far from home I was. His letter came like headlights on a late drive, flicked on in the dark of the night. I wrote Aaron to thank him for reminding me of the story I was trying to tell. I told him that, for some time now, life had felt like waking up day after day, struggling to remember who I was. His letter had given me back the stories I needed to do just that.

There are certain experiences in life that we play out in our minds years and years in advance—even the most unprepared among us—almost as if to practice them, so we're ready when we finally wake up one day and they're standing there awkwardly on our doorstep, with their shirts halfway tucked in and remnants of breakfast at the corner of their mouths. Graduation day. The first time we give ourselves to someone. The day our wife calls to say we're having a baby. But then it finally happens—we graduate, we fall in love, we find out we're with child—and it turns out to be not at all as we had sketched it out in our minds. And we realize there's no way we could have ever been prepared. Not really. Not even if we knew just how things would turn out.

When the day finally came that I found out whether we were having a baby boy or girl, I never imagined it would take place some six thousand miles away from my wife. As it turned out, that was just how it happened.

A woman in a white lab coat pressed her goo-covered wand on my wife's pregnant belly while Jen held her laptop on her chest, pointing the screen at a monitor on the wall so I could watch from my desk in Warnie's old room at the Kilns. It was nearly ten o'clock at night, and my room was just as dark as the night outside my window, with only bits of light from the ultrasound monitor illuminating the walls. Blots of white fluttered in and out against the black screen like a living, breathing Rorschach test, keeping rhythm with our baby's heartbeat.

With eyes scrunched, and my head tilted just to the side, I could finally make out a small head and spine, reclining in the water-filled home of Jen's belly. Laughter spilled out of me, uncontrollably. A smile tore its way across my face.

"Here's the head," the woman said, as if she were reading the weather report, circling our baby's melon with a digital pen. "And here's the spine," she continued, now tracing the arch of our baby's back.

More laughter. And then, a few tears. Little white arms and legs made subtle swimming movements against the black waters, and a white heart beat like a butterfly's wings inside a tiny cave of a chest.

After a couple of quiet minutes, the woman told us our baby was being stubborn.

"She must be mine," Jen said. I laughed. And then, after a few more moments, the woman asked if we were ready to find out what we were having.

"Yes," we said in one voice, even over so many miles.

"Well . . ." the woman said, with a brief pause. "You're having a baby girl!"

I erupted into laughter again. Loud, gut laughter. And I began clapping as if my home team had just won the World Series.

Jen turned the laptop screen around to face me. Her eyes were narrow slits, and I cannot now remember a time I have ever seen her so happy.

"Congratulations, hon!" I said, still grinning a wide, watermelon-slice grin. "We're having a baby girl!"

"Congratulations to you, too," Jen said, in a much cooler, more collected voice than mine, her eyes still scrunched together.

And then, my screen went black. We lost connection. My laughter turned to sobbing and I sat alone in the darkness of my room, holding my warm, wet face in my hands.

12

Decisions

An Unexpected Turn

"If one cannot be pedantic now, when can one?" Spud said to me with a smile from his seat on the couch across from mine. I wondered if he was picking up on the impatience boiling in my gut. I wondered if my thinly veiled frustration wasn't so thinly veiled.

We were sitting in his office at St. Peter's College at the time, overlooking the green cloister in Oxford's city center. A long winter stuck to the tree just beyond the window in the form of frozen limbs, and a white, electric kettle sat in his window-sill, perhaps the room's most prized possession during a cold Oxford winter.

In addition to preparing for final exams, I had been working on wrapping up my graduating thesis: "A Proper Respect for Paganism? C. S. Lewis's Christian Apologetics in Light of Pagan Mythology." Dr. Ward—Spud—was supervising my paper, and we were going over the bloodied pages of my essay. We had already met several times, so I was surprised to find so much work still to be done. As much as I appreciated his help, each red pen stroke meant less time preparing for exams.

Turning over the last page of my essay, I was thankful to wrap up our time together on a more personal note. Spud asked about my plans for the following year. He knew about my being turned down by Oxford, and my circling questions about what I might do next.

"Are you planning to reapply?"

"I have, yes," I told him. "Though I'm not holding out hope, to be honest."

The door had closed on my application to the Oxford MSt (Master of Studies) degree, but Spud had encouraged me to apply again. Apparently, the first application deadline was not the final word on the matter. It was an early application deadline for those seeking scholarships, mostly. There was another, later deadline.

"The BA is the most competitive degree at Oxford. I'd be surprised if you don't get an offer," Spud said. "But why do you want to stay for another degree?"

Because it's Oxford, I wanted to say with shrugged shoulders, but I knew he wanted something more.

"Well, because I love it here. And because I feel like I'm only just getting started. I mean, I've been here for nearly two years now, but the degree is such a whirlwind. I'd appreciate more time to dig a bit deeper."

Spud nodded, listening patiently.

I went on to tell him that I had decided to apply to Duke Divinity School, back in the States, as well, which had surprised me just as much as him.

Earlier in the year, for some reading in an ethics tutorial, I had checked out a book written by a theologian and ethicist by the name of Stanley Hauerwas. I was not familiar with his work, but the librarian's response to his book told me I should be.

"Oh, Stanley," she said, leaning back in her chair, holding his book in her hands and smiling at the cover with a look of admiration before handing it back to me. I checked out about a dozen books a week from the Theology Faculty Library; this was the first time that had ever happened. I would soon come to share her appreciation.

Using story and characters, real and fictional, Stanley Hauerwas broke down a lot of my frustration with ethics. Where others relied on academic jargon in an endless circuit of talking past one another, he cut through the conversation like a breath of fresh air, using wit and colorful, salty language in the process. *Time* magazine had named him "America's Best Theologian" a few years before. His response to this news was that he didn't realize "best" was a theological category. And he used story, powerful story, to do his work. He'd share what it was like growing up laying brick with his father in Texas, or introduce a children's story called *Watership Down* to compare different ethical positions. Whereas others often took an abstract, clinical look at morality, he would take a much different approach. He'd say, "You want to know how to live a moral life? It's by the story you're trying to tell, and how closely you actually live in a way that looks like that story." The way he relied so much on story for his work struck a chord deep within me.

As much as I wanted to stay in Oxford for another year, reading Hauerwas's words made me want to apply to Duke, where he taught. But with exams to prepare for and the C. S. Lewis Society

Called

to manage and weekly essays to write, I simply didn't have the time. So I applied to Oxford and figured that's where we'd be. That is, until the door closed on my application to Oxford and I had to figure out what to do next. I sent off my application to Duke at the last minute—it may have actually been slightly past the last minute—along with submitting my application to Oxford's second deadline.

"Duke would be a good fit," Spud told me. "Perhaps even a better fit than Oxford."

He asked me what I would end up doing if I received an acceptance letter from both schools. I laughed out loud.

"That's a humbling thought," I told him. "But I don't see that happening. I mean, I'd be thrilled with an offer from either school, but I think it'd be such a long shot."

"Don't be so sure," Spud said. "But I'll tell you, Ryan, I don't see you as an academic in the end. Nor do I see you as a pastor. I think you will end up somewhere in the middle. There's an old quote that says, 'He who would be a leader must be a bridge.'

"It will be difficult to feel pulled in different directions, but those are the most important people. They are the channels between academics and the public."

That spring, a few theologian friends and I began meeting with Professor John Lennox, an Oxford mathematician at the end of his career. Though he had lived and taught in England for years, Professor Lennox was an Irishman by birth, with a booming accent that matched his large frame. He had studied mathematics at Cambridge some fifty years earlier, while C. S. Lewis wrapped up his own teaching career at the same university.

Interestingly, at Magdalene College, Cambridge, after spending most of his career at Magdalen College, Oxford.

Professor Lennox frequently traveled around the world to talk about Christianity and the intersection between religion and science, often using vivid analogies to help illuminate his points. Short of their polar opposite talents—Lewis's struggles with math nearly prevented him from getting into Oxford—the parallels between the two men are remarkable.

Professor Lennox was speaking at an outdoor church service in South Parks, at the foot of Headington Hill, on a Saturday evening the first time I heard him. Around a hundred people from several local churches were gathered together on the sprawling grass lawn, and Professor Lennox spoke from behind a lecturn on a low stage.

Professor Lennox quoted C. S. Lewis at one point in his talk, and he mentioned that Lewis used to walk past the park on his daily commute from his home to Magdalen College. Listening to him talk about the Christian faith with his accent and imaginative analogies, I thought that this must be something of what it had been like to hear Lewis lecture.

"First priority," he said to a small group of us in our first meeting from his office in North Oxford, "you must get to know Scripture!"

Rather pointedly, Profess Lennox told my friends and me that he thought today's theologians spend too much time studying the work of other theologians, and not enough time in the Bible.

"And secondly, you will learn," he said, leaning forward in his chair, "that which costs nothing is worth nothing."

———— ❧ ————

Amanda wrote me again that spring. She told me she had received a steady stream of "Thanks, but no thanks" emails from all the publishers we had approached. All the roads we had taken turned out to be dead ends; all our nets had come up empty. While I had little hope at this point for my writing moving forward, this news still came like a blow to my tired head.

I wrote Amanda back to thank her for the update. I told her I'd like to table this project for now, and that I had something new in mind.

Tim Keller's words had lingered in my ears. "Writing comes from experience," Tim had said over our tea, and I had been wondering how that might be true of my own writing. Douglas Gresham's matter-of-factness about sharing the pain of his own story had also stuck with me, though I was still trying to wrap my head around what it all might mean.

"Once I have a bit more time," I told Amanda, "I'd love to put some more thought to this and see where things go."

Any hopes of a future for my writing had felt dead for some time, with more pronouncements of its death still slowly trickling in. But now, there suddenly seemed to be the hint of new life, even if it was only just a passing thought.

———— ❧ ————

I didn't see much of Debbie or Jonathan those days. And when I did, it was only briefly. On their way to bed, as I was getting in for the night, or on my way out the door in the morning. Inevitably, they'd ask about Jen.

"Is she feeling any better?" Or, "Any chance Jen will be returning?"

And each time, I'd miss her a little bit more. I'd say she was starting to feel a bit better, but we just didn't know whether she'd be up for the trip. And that we'd hate for her to travel all that way and then start feeling worse again. As busy as I was preparing for exams, we both knew I'd have little time to be there for her, whereas her family was taking good care of her back home.

We talked about all of this over Skype late one night. About her being there, and my being here, and about whether she should return to England or stay put. After agreeing to think and pray over it, we had told each other we would both come to this call prepared to tell the other our decision.

"Have you been eating dinner?" Jen asked, referring to my study schedule. "Don't make me sic Debbie on you!"

"Yes," I said, as if to reassure a concerned mother. "I've been eating dinner."

We talked for a few more minutes—small talk, mostly—before the inevitable point of our call finally came up.

"So, I've been thinking about what we should do," I told Jen, eyes glued to my desk, unable even to look her in the eyes at this point. "And as much as I hate to say it . . ."

My voice trailed off and my eyes became glossy. I couldn't finish my sentence, though I didn't need to. We both knew what I was going to say.

"I know," Jen said. "I hate it, too. I hate it because I feel like a single parent being here on my own, preparing for our baby's arrival, and I hate to think about being apart even longer. . . . If you want me to come back, I will. But I think it's probably best."

I nodded without speaking, looking up now to see Jen's face on the screen in front of me. It had been months since I had kissed her good-bye, and it would be a couple more before I saw her again. Small pools blotted my desktop.

Not long after our decision, I was chatting with a friend from back home, an old coworker of mine. He asked about how we were doing, and he was surprised to hear Jen and I were apart, as spring was now in full swing.

I explained to him Jen's health situation, how bad things had gotten with her pregnancy, and about my exams study schedule. I told him we had prayed over it and come to the same conclusion: she'd stay back home, and I'd see her again after my exams.

"Dude," he interjected. "That's your choice. You can choose to prioritize or neglect her. You don't have to put your school first."

His words hit me like a sack of bricks. I had already been struggling with this decision. And as bad as it hurt, the fact that Jen and I had come to the same conclusion made me think it was the right one. But then this.

When Jen and I spoke later that night, I shared the conversation with her. She reassured me that we had come to the same conclusion, that we were in agreement, and that I wasn't neglecting her.

And yet, I still wrestled with doubt and uneasiness. I wondered if I would look back on this time many years later and regret not being there for my wife during our first pregnancy. I wondered if this degree was worth it.

I was giving fewer and fewer tours of the Kilns, doing my best to stay focused on exams. But I gave one tour on a Saturday afternoon that spring, for a woman from Illinois and her two teenage children. I was showing them around Warnie's old rooms when the mother from the group noticed the ultrasound picture on my desk.

"Is that yours?" she asked with a look of confusion, seeing me there on my own.

I hesitated for a moment before explaining our situation, how Jen and I had been living here during my second year at Oxford when we traveled home for Christmas and she became sick during her pregnancy with our first child. Staring at the ultrasound picture on my desk, I told her we had decided that it'd probably be best if she stayed near the care of her family, as difficult as it was to be so far apart for our first pregnancy.

"You know, she'll never know that you weren't there for all of this," the woman said, staring me straight in the eyes. "Your daughter, I mean. You'll get back, she'll arrive, and she'll never know."

Though she had no idea about my conversation with this old colleague of mine, she went on to tell me not to worry what others might say.

"So long as you and your wife are in agreement, don't listen to those voices. What you're doing here is important."

C. S. Lewis once said that the only reason he spent so much of his time writing and talking about the Christian faith, for the everyday, non-academic crowd, was because the theologians of his day weren't. It was not lost on him that what he was doing was unpopular with many of his colleagues. Even his good friend J. R. R. Tolkien did not think it appropriate, since Lewis was neither a priest nor a trained theologian. Apparently, Lewis thought the need more important than their concerns.

"The problem with theology today," said a professor friend of mine from Seattle, sitting on a metal folding chair in a rather Spartan room in Blackfriar's Hall, one of Oxford's small religious schools, "is that most people don't think it has anything to do with reality."

Dressed in a dark button-up shirt, with thick-framed glasses, he spoke on theology and literature. His sentences were quick and sharp, and the bare skin on the top of his head caught the ceiling lights as he spoke.

He was spending his sabbatical in Oxford, working on some writing, and enjoying the city with his wife and their three girls. I had them over to the Kilns for tea and a tour when they first arrived. With three voracious readers for daughters, they loved it.

I was sure I wouldn't be able to make it out for his talk when he had invited me a few days before—I was nearly living in the Harris Manchester library, preparing for exams around the clock—but minutes before the talk was scheduled to begin, something tugged me out of my chair and insisted I go. So I raced out of the library, hopped on my bike, and made my way to Blackfriar's Hall.

There were an unimpressive number of people scattered unevenly across the chairs placed in a circle around the room. Apart from me and one or two other theology students, the chairs were filled mostly by the Dominicans who lived and studied there, dressed in their full-length white robes. I felt very out of place in my T-shirt, faded jeans, and scuffed Converse. And I didn't realize how tired I was until I got there and struggled not only to keep pace with the lecture, but to stay awake. Fortunately, my professor-friend's words struck me like a slap to the back of the head.

"Most people don't think theology has anything to do with reality," he said. He went on to talk about how far removed most theological work is from the public's thought and conversation. He said he believed theology needed to become more imaginative. That was something that had been lost in modern works, he suggested, and he pointed to literature—to great story—as a possible fix.

I couldn't help but think of Lewis's words about the theologians of his own day.

Then one of the Dominicans spoke up. An unassuming, pale man dressed in his white robe, with a crescent-shaped hairline that circled his head just above his ears. He said something that evening that shook me awake, and has kept shaking me to this day.

"Good theology makes us *do* something."

———————— ∾ ————————

By spring of my second year, I could ride home to the Kilns with my eyes closed. The familiar journey through the high-rising stone college walls, over the arching Magdalene Bridge, up the never-ending incline of Headington Hill, past the Headington shops, all closed down for the night, across the roundabout, past the palm tree standing on the corner, and up Kilns Lane before turning into the Lewis Close cul-de-sac. And many times, as exhausted as I was from preparing for exams, I nearly did.

But there was one night in which my eyes were anything but closed, when I found myself laughing out loud at the joke of it all.

I was working on revisions earlier in the day at Harris Manchester when I received a note from the Oxford Graduate Studies office. And I knew, immediately, it was the news of their decision. Hesitantly, I opened the email. The first sentence confirmed my suspicion, directing me to open an attached letter. It seemed so painstakingly unnecessary, like an endless series of Russian nesting dolls. My heart sank as I opened the attachment, even before I had read the first sentence. I had an overwhelming feeling that once again I had not been offered a position.

After receiving the initial note of rejection, a general malaise for Oxford had begun to make its home within me. That which I had so loved about the city before was replaced, almost overnight, with resentment. The smiles on the faces of other students, the libraries overflowing with books from floor to ceiling, the bustling city center, all things I loved before, now were only reminders of my rejection. Quite suddenly, I felt like an outsider to the club I was still inside. I began to tell myself that Oxford really wasn't all that great anyway, and that it wasn't for me after all. Like the girl who was all but perfect in your eyes before she turns you down, who tells you, "It's not *you*, it's *me*," and you try to fool yourself into believing her.

She's really not my type anyhow, you begin to tell yourself. *Too tall.* Or, *Too short. And she pops her knuckles when she's anxious, remember?* And you make half-hearted comments to your friends about how you knew, deep down, it would never have worked out. Searching desperately for their support, you say something like, "Besides, she wears those big, gaudy watches."

And then your good friend—since he's a good friend—scrunches his brow, nods his head, and says something like, "Hmmm . . . Yeah. Girls with big watches? Never trust 'em."

All the while, you're not-so-secretly feeling sorry for yourself, and they're not-so-secretly feeling sorry for you. Because you both know, deep down, you'd give anything to be with that girl, and you die a little inside thinking about her rejection.

That's how Oxford's note of rejection had felt to me. I had written the story of our future together in my mind, and then I watched as it all fell through my hands. Ashamed for even dreaming of such a story, I quickly began to pretend as though I didn't care. But I did. I cared very much. Which made this letter so unbelievable.

> Dear Mr. Ryan Pemberton,
> I am delighted to inform you that your application for admission to the University of Oxford as a graduate student has been successful. . . . Our admissions round is incredibly competitive, and we would like to congratulate you most warmly on your success.

After telling myself Oxford's rejection wasn't a big deal for so long, this note made all those thoughts fade away like lines to a play I no longer needed to rehearse. Oxford had broken my heart, but boy was she beautiful. And now, there she was, standing on my front doorstep, asking if we could give it another shot.

I wrote Jen to share the news with her. I couldn't wait to get back to the Kilns that night and see her reaction on Skype. I also wrote Duke, to check in on the status of my application. Before the day was through, someone at Duke wrote back to apologize for the wait. Their letter had been delayed in the mail, they told me, assuring me I should be receiving it soon. They went on to let me know I had a place at Duke waiting for me the following year.

My laughter tore through the cold air as I rode back to the Kilns late that evening, surprising me as it slipped out unexpected. *A kid like me,* I thought to myself, *offered a place at Oxford* and *Duke.* It seemed too good to be true.

It reminded me of that old story of God showing up and telling the childless, nearly one-hundred year old Abraham that he would be the father of many nations—that from his descendants would come not only nations, but kings. It reminded me of how Abraham fell flat on his face in the dirt from laughing so hard, looking around with tear-soaked eyes, as if to ask, "Is anyone else getting this?" And, just to make clear that God, indeed, has a sense of humor, God went ahead and told Abraham to name his soon-to-be child Isaac, which translates in English as, "He laughs." The joke wasn't lost on Abraham. Nor was the humor of it all lost on God. He's been surprising the world with his topsy-turvy humor ever since.

I rode up Headington Hill sometime later, late one evening after a full day's studies, thinking back to Spud's question he had asked me at his office at St. Peter's College, about what I'd do if I received an offer from both schools. And I remembered how I had laughed in response, brushing off any suggestion that that might actually happen. *You're a real crack-up, Spud,* I had thought. But now, now we had a major decision on our hands.

Major decisions ruin me. I turn them over and over in my head endlessly, wishing I could escape them, wishing I could get a bit of a reprieve. But I never do. Not until they're decided.

I usually like to turn to friends and mentors with these kinds of decisions, to ask for their advice. But most of those I'd normally turn to were back in the States. I found myself wishing I could catch up with my good friend Doug over breakfast and ask for his advice. I found myself wishing Jen and I were together, in person, so I could see it in her face and hear it in her voice when I asked where she thought we should be.

When it came to our decision to leave home, careers, and community for Oxford, I tried to imagine how I'd look back on this decision years later, and what I'd think about my decision to stay, or my decision to go. And I tried to do the same again here, two years later. I found myself trying to imagine how I might explain this decision to our baby girl years from now, when she came to me asking for advice with a major decision she was facing herself.

Prayer has been priceless when it has come to the biggest decisions of my life. Usually, any answer to prayer takes a while. But prayer—candid, relentless, heartfelt prayer, the kind of prayer that comes from deep within the gut and is heaved up to God—has helped me move forward at those times when my questions are faced with nothing more than vague notions, shrugged shoulders, and dead ends.

I remember when I was in college, after Jen and I had been dating for several years, and we had begun to talk about marriage. I was scared out of my wits.

Even though I knew I always wanted to get married some-day, and even though I could not imagine life without Jen, the thought of getting married scared me. I had seen it go wrong many times in my family. I had grown up with the remnants of its destruction, trying to live among its wreckage as a young boy, and knowing I'd do anything to avoid making the same mistakes when I had a chance. And so the idea of entering into marriage, with even the slightest possibility of divorce, was enough to make me think twice.

At the time, it was all I could think about. I stressed about it. I didn't want to make the wrong decision. I didn't want to ask Jen to make a deal with me I would break. I didn't want to make a disaster out of our relationship. Or her life. I was so scared. At the same time, I could not imagine my life without her. I was stuck.

So I prayed. For months I prayed, asking, *Is she the one?* And I remember on one summer evening, after going to bed with this decision heavy on my mind, being awakened by a thought. Awakened by words not yet audible enough to hear, but loud enough to know they were there: *The answer will come trickling down.*

And then, a fluttering noise caused me to lift my head from my pillow and look around my room. It was the fluttering noise of wings beating the air. And it took me a moment to locate it, in the dark, with my eyes still adjusting.

The sound had come from a small piece of paper now lying still on my floor, which had taken flight from its previous position on my desk with the help of the oscillating fan that stood at the foot of my bed.

A piece of paper, simple enough, floating in the air. But what was on the paper was enough to make my hair stand on end. It was a note I had written late one evening several months earlier, with three bullet points.

- Her smile, which can create a good day out of the worst days.
- She's going to make the world's best mother.
- She has the biggest heart of anyone I know.

Late one evening, several months earlier, I had written out the things I appreciated most about Jen, for no particular reason. They had come to me while driving home late one night, and I promised myself I would write them out as soon as I got home. And after sleeping with my fan on for more than a month, on this particular evening, this is when the paper note got my attention.

Though it's hard to put your finger on those moments wherein the transcendent-temporal divide is breached, when the fluttering movement of the Holy Spirit casts itself into the mundane reality of our lives, I was pretty sure, in those early morning hours, God had been there. Fluttering into the silence of my room, stirring me awake, and pulling me into his flow.

The next day, on a late-summer afternoon from a leather sofa in their living room, I asked Jen's parents for their permission to ask Jen to graft her life to mine in marriage.

When the answer to prayer finally comes, it may not always be so dramatic, of course. Most times it won't be. Nor is it likely to be quite so tangible. Most times we don't have anything we can hold in our hands and say, "*See!*" Most times we have to take a step, leaving our sure footing, in faith that when we do, we're doing so because that's where God is leading us.

Of course, it is at this point that someone will say, with a grin and a wink, "That, my friend, is what we call a coincidence."

And to such people, there is only one response: You're right. That is what we call coincidence. Coincidence; miracle. To-may-to; to-mah-to.

Am I sure that the whispered words and fluttering note were a miracle and not a coincidence? I am not so sure I know the difference. Nor am I sure that the sudden and complete peace found in that moment is any less a miracle than any other detail of the experience.

So I continue to pray.

I began to pray as I pushed my way up the long slope of Headington Hill late one night that spring in Oxford, leg over leg, asking for clarity in this decision. Asking that God might show us whether we should stay or go. That he might show us his will in it all. I prayed on that same hill where many years before C. S. Lewis once sat in a double-decker bus making his way back home, wrestling with his own decision: whether he ought to let God in, or keep the divine at arm's length. And by the time I made it home to the Kilns that evening, I had my answer.

13

Culmination

The Proper Rewards

Idou! the word appeared in my mind with a jolt, shaking me awake from my sleep. *Idou!* the word came again.

With my eyes still closed, I reached across to my nightstand, grabbed my cell phone, and pulled it close to my face. It was not yet four thirty, but I felt as though I was being ushered out of bed on this Easter morning, strangely, in Greek.

Idou! Behold! Look! The translation came surprisingly easy at such an ungodly hour. But it didn't stop there. *I am doing something new here. Come see!*

I showered while the rest of the house slept. I dressed, then stepped outside into the dark morning. The birds were chirping as I climbed onto my bike. Early as it was, the noise of the birds' songs made it seem as if all of nature was waking up and attesting to this new thing God did, and was doing, on Easter morning.

As I rode to the city center in the chilly morning air, I remembered the scene in the Bible when the women went to the tomb that first Easter Sunday to pay their respects to Jesus, and I wondered if they had heard the same words that morning. I wondered if God had awakened them with the sudden, shocking words: *Behold! Look! Come and see what I have done.*

A smile spread across my face as I rode past Magdalene Tower, feeling as though I was taking part in a two-thousand-year-old celebration. Riding through the eerily empty streets, I remembered how packed High Street was on May Day at this same hour the previous year. When students stumbled out of their colleges, many wearing only their underwear and a necktie, and carrying with them the last remnants of their drink from the party the night before.

I thought about the crowds that gathered for this May Day event, and I wondered where they all were on this Easter morning.

How can you possibly be sleeping at such a time as this? I thought to myself.

About a dozen of us gathered at the top of the oldest tower in Oxford early Easter morning, in the dark. There were mostly gray-haired couples dressed in puffy jackets, along with a younger couple around my age, and a thirtysomething father with his young, floppy-haired, sleepy-eyed son.

Shortly after we began, a man, whom I could smell before I could see, appeared from the staircase, still wearing the scent of his drink like a cheap cologne. Taking his place beside the young dad, this man's guilty smile soon faded and his face went pale as he looked out across the 360-degree view of the city's rooftops and steeples. A moment later, he turned and disappeared back down the staircase. Several smiles were exchanged as the vicar, a woman with salt-and-pepper hair, began reading from Matthew's gospel. The pale-faced man soon regained his courage, reappearing a few minutes later, deciding to brave the rooftop service after all.

We sang several hymns, we prayed, and then we took communion, tearing bite-sized pieces from a baguette, and taking turns drinking from a silver goblet of red wine.

By the time we were done, the sun had just risen, casting light on the formerly dark city. We left the church tower as the city awoke.

The buds burst into blossoms of white and pink around Oxford that spring, filling the air with an extravagant fragrance of new life. The formerly gaunt trees were now dressed in brilliant colors, reaching out to those passing by, as if to hand out bouquets. Flowerbeds seemed to sprout up overnight, transforming the earthy, black-brown ground into beautiful fields of blues and yellows and reds. The gloomy winter skies turned from gray to blue, crisscrossed by white airplane trails, and punts carrying young couples glided lazily down the River Cherwell, the riverbank lined with students lying on their backs in the green grass with books blanketing their faces.

As if to reflect nature's awakening from its winter slumber, the news from Oxford and Duke filled my tired frame with renewed energy. Exams were just around the corner, and with them, the thrill of knowing that it wouldn't be long before I'd once again be holding Jen in my arms as we prepared for the arrival of our baby girl.

It was the last week before exams began when I was cycling from the Kilns to the Harris Manchester library and noticed the palm tree standing at the foot of Kilns Lane. It was standing tall and healthy, and its fronds were green and thick, waving to me in the breeze as I rode past.

———————————— ❧ ————————————

Jen and I were still separated by miles of earth and ocean when it finally came time to decide what we'd be doing the following year. Given how far apart we were, I was worried about how we were ever going to come to a decision.

Usually, our decisions involved late-night conversations, prayer, and more conversations over coffee as we started our day. Given our separation, this wasn't an option. We'd catch up as much as possible at night, but between my study schedule and her health, we weren't able to talk nearly as much as we liked.

So we set ourselves a date when we'd both come to a decision and let one another know what we were thinking. I pulled Jen up on Skype and persuaded her to show me a profile view of her six-months-pregnant belly. She stood, sheepishly, and turned for me to see.

"She kicked for me the other night," Jen told me with wide eyes. "I was turning over in bed when I felt it. She must not have liked that I woke her. I wish you could have felt it."

"Me too, hon."

We spoke a bit more about our baby girl, about things Jen was hoping we could pick out together when I got home, and about getting my help putting together our baby's bed. And then I asked what she was thinking about our decision. Though I had not yet told her, I knew where I thought we were supposed to be, struck in a moment of clarity on my bike ride back to the Kilns several weeks earlier.

I was relieved when her answer matched mine. I wrote Duke right away to tell them my decision; Oxford could wait until after exams.

"So how are you feeling about exams, man?" Don King asked from his seat across the dining room table at the Kilns. Not the boxing promoter Don King, with the wild hair, but the North Carolina English professor who taught on C. S. Lewis and wrote on Joy's poetry, with the much more tame hair. Don was visiting Oxford that spring. He was dressed in a T-shirt, blue jeans, and bright-red Chuck Taylors, and he spoke in a quiet, cool tone. Debbie sat at the opposite end of the table, beside a burly American pastor from New Mexico with his sixteen-year-old daughter, who were visiting the Kilns that weekend. And all of those seated around the table were now staring at me, dressed in my Hogwarts-like black gown.

I imagined I'd hardly be able to sit down and enjoy the breakfast of fruit and yogurt and granola Debbie had prepared for me on this morning. But only hours away from sitting the first of my seven Oxford exams, I was at peace.

I had taken a rare break from preparing for exams the night before and joined a couple of friends for dinner in the city center: John and John, both tall and athletic, both much sharper than me, both with long, floppy brown hair, and both of whom were also preparing for theology exams. It was a time to come alongside and encourage one another.

I had confessed to John and John—both of whom, though kind as could be, always made me feel a bit shorter than normal, and not nearly so smart—that I had been feeling quite sick about the whole thing. About exams. About knowing my entire time at Oxford was weighing on these final exams, and waking up in the early morning hours by the reoccurring nightmare that after months of studying, I would not be able to recall anything to scratch down on paper when it finally came time to sit my exams.

John and John both nodded their heads in agreement from the living room of John Ash's home, where we were dining on overcooked store-bought pizza and steamed broccoli. John Ash, almost indistinguishable from John Adams—except, perhaps, for having slightly less brown, floppy hair—spoke up.

"I've got to tell you, I've been struggling with the same thing. And you know what I've been telling myself? I've been thinking, when we're worshipping in the Lord's presence millions and millions of years from now, I don't think anyone's going to stop what they're doing, turn around, and ask, 'Hey, remind me, how'd you do on your exams again?'"

"That's right," John Adams spoke up with a laugh, feigning a cringed face and pointing backwards over his shoulder with his thumb. "Oh, that bad? Shouldn't you be back there a bit?"

When Don asked how I was doing the next morning over breakfast, I shared this story with him, Debbie, and the American pastor and his daughter.

"As much as these exams matter for my degree, I know they're far from everything. That makes this an entirely different ball game for me."

"That's exactly the right perspective, man," Don said, his lip curling up at the corner. The American pastor smiled and nodded. Debbie stared back at me from the opposite end of the table wearing a reassuring smile, perhaps with a little pride even, knowing how many hours I had put into preparing for exams, all of the late nights, and the dreadful experience of doing it all so far from Jen.

I smiled and thanked Don. I liked that he called me "man."

Walter sent me a note that morning, which I received on my bus ride to the city center.

Dear Ryan,
God bless you, dear friend! I'll be praying for you while you endure Schools, and I feel sure you'll do well.

Meanwhile, I want you to know that you will go down in history as one of the Very Best Presidents the C. S. Lewis Society has ever had! You could not have done it better. God bless you.
Yours,
Walter

The students stood under a white canopy, all dressed in their Sub Fusc, young men and women in black gowns over black suits and dresses and white shirts, buzzing like an apple orchard in the heat of summer. To one side of the canopy, a line of people— parents and friends and police officers—waved from the street just beyond the iron gate. To the other side of the canopy stood a tall, ominous building: Oxford's exam schools.

I stood beside John and John early on this Saturday morning, both looking disgustingly cool and collected, while I did my best not to look as though I was going to throw up. Students flipped through their flash cards in their final minutes before exams.

Some brave souls danced in a circle. Others paced nervously. And then, a proctor gave us instructions to enter the schools, and we funneled in like sheep to the slaughter.

We walked a long corridor and began to climb a stairway toward the second floor, where our exams would be held.

"Take note of this, Ryan," John Adams said. "This will be the only time you will walk up a marble staircase to take an exam."

"I hope so," I told him.

One of the girls in front of us whispered in a British accent to a friend that she thought she was going to pee herself.

We gathered in a cavernous room, filled with several long, neat lines of desks, each with an exam facedown and a name in the corner. After several minutes of searching, I finally found the desk bearing my name and took my seat. The room was a sea of students, salt-and-peppered in their black and white Sub Fusc. There must have been nearly two hundred of us crammed together by the time everyone found their seat. Tall portraits, taller than me, hung in ornate golden frames, between oversized, arched windows.

Examiners dressed in academic gowns stood at the front of the room. In the middle stood a large, pale man whose neck dangled like a turkey. He announced the detailed instructions for the exams, mentioning several times not to turn over our exams before we were instructed to do so. And then, five minutes later, in a flash of paper and pens scratching, we were off. Three hours later, I was wandering through the Oxford city center in my Hogwarts-like robe, frazzled, with a half-smile. It was the first time in months I had felt as though I just might survive.

After taking a half day to witness Tobias's baptism with Olli and Salla and a number of friends at the front of St. Andrew's

Church in North Oxford, I sat three more exams in a twenty-four hour period. By the time I was done with my fourth exam, I could not tell John Adams which exam I had just sat. I simply stood there outside of the Exam Schools building, staring blankly back at him for a long, silent fifteen seconds.

"It's okay," John said with a laugh. "Don't worry about it. I'm sure you did fine."

After a half day off before my next exam, I was seated at my second-story desk in the Harris Manchester library, preparing to take my fifth exam—patristics, which I was feeling good about. As I was studying, however, I realized that if I had to make the walk to Exams Schools that day, and if I had to take my seat in the great hall of desks and students dressed in their Sub Fusc again, I was sure I would paint the floor with the contents of my stomach.

I talked to someone at the college about it, and after a quick phone call to the local doctor's office—who sounded as though she was used to the routine of sick Oxford students during exams—I had a faxed doctor's note excusing me from taking my exams in the Exams Schools. I would be allowed to sit the exam from college that afternoon, which instantly calmed my churning stomach. A lone examiner and I sat in an otherwise empty room in college, where I skated my way through the exam in the allotted three hours—even smiling, at times.

After finishing my sixth exam the next morning, thumb and forefinger now completely numb, and struggling to think straight, I had a full twenty-four hours before my next, and final, exam. I was studying at the desk in my room at the Kilns that afternoon when a knock came at the door.

"Come in."

"Oh, hullo," Jonathan said, opening the door, and looking surprised to see me. "I thought I might have heard you here."

"Yeah, I'm spoiling myself by studying from home for my last exam."

"Good idea. Well, I thought I'd check to see if you have dinner plans."

"Oh, no. I hadn't thought about it, to be honest."

"Good. I picked up a roast from the market this weekend, intending to make dinner one night for you during your exams, but I'm afraid I've been busy and haven't had a chance. Might this evening be okay?"

"That sounds perfect."

"Okay, great," he said with a smile, closing the door behind him.

I wandered into the Kilns later that evening, and I was met by a wave of delicious smells.

"Almost there," Jonathan said to me as I entered, looking up from his work at the stove, wearing a washrag draped over his shoulder. "Would you like me to bring you a plate when it's ready?"

"Actually," I told him, "if you don't mind, it would be nice if we could have dinner together."

"Of course," Jonathan said, visibly surprised by my request.

I had rarely taken a break over the past few months to share a meal, and everyone living at the Kilns had noticed my absence.

After I had all but licked my plate clean, Jonathan surprised me with a berry tart he had prepared. The top of the tart had the words, "Good luck, Ryan!" spelled out in blueberries and raspberries.

I woke up the next morning and dressed for my last exam, feeling as though it was my birthday.

By the time I took my seat in the Exams Schools that afternoon, I had become so familiar with the routine that I was mouthing the words to the examiner's instructions. But then something unfamiliar caught my eye. It was Philip, my tutor for modern theology. This was the first and only time I had seen him supervising an exam.

My last exam was on modern theology, which I was feeling most confident about. I had looked forward to Philip's tutorials each week, and I always left feeling good about our conversation. It's funny, given how dreadful I had felt about exams, that I was actually looking forward to this one.

I smiled, seeing Philip at the front of the room, dressed in his academic robe. He smiled back at me with a wink. And then the examiner gave the go-ahead. I flipped open the exam workbook and began.

Less than three hours later, I put a period at the end of my last sentence, closed up my exam book, and looked up at the clock, only to notice I still had several minutes left. It was the first time that had happened. This exam was what all of my previous exams could only ever dream of being. Philip noticed I had finished early and shone me another smile. I gave him a nod and a wink, knowing that was it. It was finished.

It was then that I recalled something C. S. Lewis wrote many years ago:

> The proper rewards are not simply tacked on to the activity for which they are given, but are the activity itself in consummation.

Seated there in the middle of this room with enormous portraits in huge, gold frames, looking around at all of these students anxiously scratching the final few sentences into their exam books; thinking about the endless hours I had spent in the library; the Greek flash cards I had written up and gone over and over and over; the late nights of studying that would regularly stretch into the early morning hours; I suddenly realized what Lewis had meant.

This moment, in the space between all my revisions work and the clock telling me I was now finished, before being draped in silly string and glitter and shouts of "Congratulations!" and hugs, knowing I had given it my all, *this* moment was my reward.

After a day of sleeping and eating as much as I could, I phoned my mom for the first time in months. I hadn't heard her voice since before I had begun preparing for exams. She was surprised to hear mine on the other end.

"Hey, Mom."

"Ryan? . . . Hey, hon! How are you?!"

"I'm good. I'm good, thanks. Hey, I wanted to call you to tell you I'm done. I did it. I finished my exams and I'm done."

I could hear the tears in my mom's voice as she told me how proud she was of me, and how happy she was to hear I was now done. She knew how rough the whole process had been on me. She would regularly send me notes to let me know she was praying for me. And to remind me to take time to eat.

I thanked her for her prayers, and for sharing in my excitement. And then I went on.

"And I wanted to tell you, Mom, I'm coming home. We decided to take the Duke offer. I'll be moving back to the States. To stay."

She screamed at that point. Not a restrained, I'm-going-to-show-you-how-excited-I-am fake scream, but a real, loud, surprised scream. The kind of scream that escapes before you have time to hold it back.

I moved the phone away from my ear and smiled.

My eyes opened and my mind blinked to life much earlier than I expected at the start of the first week after exams. I hadn't been able to sleep nearly as much as I imagined I would after exams had finished. My mind was still racing, going over names and dates on an endless, uncontrollable cycle, and I struggled to stay in bed for more than seven hours at a time.

I took a seat at my desk at the Kilns and began stretching my fingers. My thumb and forefinger were still numb from all the writing. Opening my laptop, I began typing the email I never thought I would send. I wrote to thank Oxford for their offer of a place in the master's program for the following year, and to let them know I wouldn't be accepting it.

Philip came to my mind as I typed, knowing he would have been my advisor for the degree. And as difficult as it was—knowing I was giving up on the opportunity to continue my work with him, saying good-bye to so many people I knew and loved, and bidding farewell to the school of my dreams—I knew that were it not for the hand of God in all of this, there's no way I would have ever written such an email. Knowing, in fact, that I would have tackled myself before I ever hit Send.

It felt surreal to be turning down the university I had dreamt of coming to for so long. It felt so strange to be writing these words, after being here, and after falling in love with Oxford long after it had only been a dream. It felt silly, really. And yet, I did so in confidence, even as the tears welled in the corners of my eyes. I did so knowing how difficult it would be to say good-bye to this place that had been so unbelievable that it made all my dreams feel so thin and frail in comparison, because Jen and I were sure God had something else in store. Even though we couldn't yet see just what that was, or how things were going to work out.

I think sometimes that's a sign of the Lord's work in our lives, those unexplainable moments when things turn out completely different than we would have thought, when the current of life moves us in a new, unexpected direction, and we cannot believe how well it fits. I think that can be a sign of God's patient, intentional hands molding our hearts. Those moments when you can say, *I would not be doing this, I would not be here now, were I left to my own devices. But here I am, and it feels right, somehow.*

Debbie was preparing a cup of tea when I wandered into the kitchen after sending the email.

"Heyyy, good morning," she said in a loud, cheery voice. "You're already looking better, Ryan. You know that?"

I had not realized how much revisions had affected me physically, until people began pointing it out on the other side of exams. I had not noticed that my hair hadn't been cut in months and my pants no longer fit.

"Yeah? Thanks, Debbie. I feel better. It's nice to sleep again."

"I bet!"

"So I just wrote Oxford's grad committee," I told Debbie as I pulled out one of the knee-high stools and took a seat beside her.

"Oh wow. . . . How are you feeling about it?"

"Well, I don't know," I said with a laugh, rubbing my fingers through the hair on the back of my head. "I mean, it's just, it feels like a dream, to be honest. Kind of surreal, you know? I know it's the right decision, I know this is where God is leading us, but I just never imagined . . ."

Debbie looked at me with a serious face and nodded as my voice trailed off. Then, a smile began to curl the corner of her lips upward.

"God is so good, Ryan," she said, smiling proudly, and shaking her head.

"Mmmm, yeah," I looked at Debbie and nodded, with my brow lowered, still unclear why she had just said this.

But then she continued, still preparing her cup of tea as she talked.

"God closed this door to Oxford for you at first, to direct you toward the path he had for you. And then, when that was clear, he went ahead and gave you the acceptance you wanted here after all."

She finished her sentence, smiling at me. "He is so good."

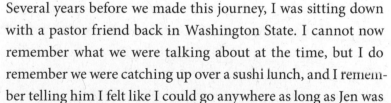

Several years before we made this journey, I was sitting down with a pastor friend back in Washington State. I cannot now remember what we were talking about at the time, but I do remember we were catching up over a sushi lunch, and I remember telling him I felt like I could go anywhere as long as Jen was with me. I told him I felt like she was my family, that she was now my home, and that was all that I needed.

It wasn't long afterword that I began to feel as though God was calling us to leave home and the career I loved to return to school, to study theology, so as to bring my education and writing together in a way that might help others see Christ more clearly. I had fallen head-over-heels in love with Oxford years before, reading Lewis, and I remember it was at that point that I said to God in prayer, *Okay, I'm willing to leave home and my career to study theology, but* only *if it's at Oxford.*

And now, at the end of my time in Oxford, I wondered if this wasn't, in some small way, God saying, *This is what I'd like you to do: give up your dream girl. First your wife, then Oxford. And make me your dream.*

While Oxford is not a bad thing to love, and while it'd be crazy to suggest I ought not love my wife, neither of them can be everything to me. Not in the way God is. And somewhere along the way, I had become confused about that. I wondered if this entire journey had not been, in a rather complicated way, a process of God leaving me with nothing but him, so that I might finally see that he is my home.

My friend, Professor Steve—the one who confessed to me in a whisper that returning to Oxford always feels a bit like returning to Narnia—once gave a talk in which he said he thinks every story has one common theme: home. And most times, he said, all stories are, in the end, about returning home.

I remember listening to him talk and thinking, *I really like this guy, but that's crazy.* And then, a little while later, when I had stopped shaking my head and laughing to myself, I began to think he might not be so crazy after all.

14

Memories

How could I forget a fairy tale?

The last tour I gave of the Kilns fell on a Saturday afternoon, and I nearly made it all the way through the tour before I realized it was my last tour. I did my best to fight back the tears that tried to wrestle their way into the corners of my eyes.

I told all the familiar stories I had now told hundreds of times before. Laughs came at all the old jokes. I pointed out all the same photos along the way, and answered the familiar questions when they came. And even though I had done it all before so many times, I still loved it. All of it.

We concluded the tour in a room at the end of the hallway at the front of the house. The room where Lewis stayed at the end of his life, when he could no longer make it up and down the stairs to his old bedroom.

Crowded into the tight room, I told the group that the room where they were standing was the room where Lewis had passed away, just after taking his tea at four in the afternoon, on

November 22, 1963. A few people let out an audible gasp. One man pointed out that that was the same day President Kennedy was assassinated.

"That's right," I told him. "And the same day Aldous Huxley passed, author of *A Brave New World*."

And then I went on to tell them a story from the end of Lewis's life. One of my favorites.

The story involved Maureen, who was Mrs. Moore's daughter and sister to Paddy Moore (Lewis's good friend who had entered the pact with Lewis before the Great War). Maureen had lived with Lewis and her mother, Janie Moore, at the Kilns for years before she married and moved out. Long after she had moved out of the Kilns, toward the very end of Lewis's life, she received word that several men in her family had passed away and she would be inheriting a castle in Scotland, along with the title Lady Dunbar of Hempriggs.

Her mother had told Maureen as a young girl that there was a slight possibility that one day this could happen, but neither Janie nor Maureen ever thought it would. But it did happen, like a fairy tale.

I shared a story Walter had told me during my first visit to the Kilns, about the time when J. R. R. Tolkien paid a visit to Lewis at the end of his life. Lewis was in such bad shape at the time, slipping in and out of consciousness, that Tolkien came and left without Lewis even noticing.

Maureen showed up to see Lewis not long after Tolkien. Walter greeted her at the door and explained what had happened with Tolkien, so that she would be prepared before she saw him. She thanked Walter for letting her know, and she insisted that she'd still like to see him.

"Hello, Jack, it's me, Maureen," she said as she entered the room, unsure whether he'd even know she was there.

Much to her surprise, he did.

"You mean, Lady Dunbar of Hempriggs," he said, speaking up.

Not knowing whether or not he would even know she was there, Maureen was completely taken aback.

"Oh Jack, how could you remember such a thing at a time like this?"

"On the contrary," he said. "How could I forget a fairy tale?"

And standing there in the middle of this small, packed room, with the afternoon sun cascading across the wardrobe and the bed, it was as if I was hearing the story for the first time.

How could I forget a fairytale, indeed, I thought to myself.

––––––––––– ❧ –––––––––––

My last week in Oxford was filled with good-byes, and many tears. I stopped into Harris Manchester one last time to pick up my books and notes from the library, piled high like towers on the desk from which I had worked for the past two years. The one with the brass nameplate that reads, "Roger Bannister." Before picking up my things to leave, I stopped to stare out the second-story window one last time, taking in the view of the Oxford rooftops, lined with shingles and chimneys poking into the pale-blue afternoon sky. And I found myself overwhelmed to think I would no longer be returning here to take in this view, day after day.

With a pile of folders and notes heavy in my arms, I made my way downstairs and stopped just before walking out the double doors. I set my things down on a large wood desk and made a point to say good-bye to Sue, the librarian. She noticed me coming and greeted me with a sympathetic face. I stooped down low and wrapped her in a tight hug.

"Oh, Ryan. You're a big softie, aren't you?"

I nodded, and shook slightly, knowing she could feel the warmth of my tears on the side of her head as we hugged.

"You're making the right decision, Ryan," she told me, now holding my shoulders at arm's length. "And you're going to be a great father."

My buddy, Tom, and I were walking back from the pub late one evening, back to the Kilns, when he began to list out all that had happened to us since we first arrived in Oxford. All the ups and downs of our journey.

"If you would have written about your time before you arrived . . ." he started to ask.

". . . It would not have been as incredible as all of this," I said, finishing his sentence.

The garden in front of the Kilns was filled with friends the following day, on a sunny June afternoon. The smell of hamburgers and sausages floated through the air amid the sound of children's laughter as I shared laughs and hugs with friends who I had met along the way. Friends who I did not know when I would see again. Olli and Salla and their two beautiful, white-haired boys. David, my American New Testament tutor who told me arriving in England is a bit like finding everything in your house rotated ninety degrees. Emily, the friend from college with whom I first shared that I escape to writing as therapy. Rosie, who shared with me the fact that she wanted to make beautiful things. Even Cole came—he was now working on his doctorate in Scotland, and I had not seen him in months.

At the end of the evening, most of the people had gone home and it was just a few of us talking around the dining room table inside the Kilns. It was less than twenty-four hours before I was scheduled to fly home. I asked an Argentinean friend of mine, Ignacio, how he said good-bye to so many friends year after year.

Ignacio was one of the few Oxford graduates to have actually been offered a place to stay on and teach after finishing his degree, and I knew he had seen many friends come and go throughout the years.

"It's still really difficult," he told me in his thick Argentinean accent. "Not with everyone, of course, but with those who get into your heart."

He paused for a moment, and then continued.

"It took me a couple of years to learn this, but memories are not people, Ryan. When you realize that, you realize that life changes, but those people are still there, and that makes saying good-bye not nearly so difficult."

The next day, Debbie prepared a breakfast in honor of my last morning at the Kilns. It was a beautiful, warm morning, and she suggested we push some of the wood tables together in the garden and dine outside. It was just the three of us there at the Kilns that morning: Cole, Debbie, and me, and I found myself thinking how much the end of my time in Oxford looked like the beginning.

After Debbie had prayed, we made small talk as we enjoyed our eggs and toast and fresh orange juice. Leaves on the trees danced to the sound of birds chirping, and I glanced at my watch every few minutes, watching my time in Oxford drift away.

Even the old familiar trees, with their leaves dancing gently, seemed to be saying good-bye. And the chorus of birds singing their familiar songs seemed to be saying good-bye. And the three of us, sitting there talking about nothing in particular, we were saying good-bye in our own little way. Even though we never used the word.

"Are you going to make it to my performance in August?" Cole asked Debbie between bites.

"I hope to, yes," she said. "But I need to add it to my diary. I'm learning that my time here goes much more quickly than I realize."

They continued talking about Cole's upcoming show and I took a sip of my orange juice, smiling at the truth of her words.

I left Oxford the third week of June, after two years and many heavy-hearted good-byes. I spent most of the ten-hour flight to Washington State with a smile on my face and tears in my eyes— sometimes happy tears and sometimes sad, but mostly happy. I couldn't wait to hold Jen in my arms, to see her beautiful smile that first stole my heart more than ten years earlier, to feel her lips on mine, and to place my hands on her now very pregnant belly. I couldn't wait to feel our baby girl kick for the first time, a short five weeks before she was due to arrive.

When I first saw my wife again, she was dragging a piece of luggage off the conveyor belt. It was just over fifty pounds, and she was nearly eight months pregnant. No matter. It needed to be done, so she'd do it.

Jen didn't see me, but I saw her. I began laughing from some fifty feet away. My feet slapped hurriedly against the tiled floor, weaving through other travelers. Slowing my pace as I finally reached her, so as to surprise her, I placed my hand on her hand, now sitting atop my luggage. She swung her head around with such speed I thought she might take a swing at me. In a moment, her face went from a frantic "Who are you?!" to a relieved "There you are!"

Tears warmed my cheeks as we embraced. Her belly, so full of life, stretched out between us. I placed my hands on either side of it, fingers fully extended, and we exchanged smiles, Jen and me. My gaze then returned to the gift I held in my hands: our baby girl, reclining in her mother's womb.

Jen and I awoke around four o'clock the next morning, covered in white linens and smiles. We were too excited about being together again to sleep. She'd lay her head in the corner of my shoulder, and it felt just like home. And I was relieved because, during those long, dark, hard months apart, which often felt like a cold winter storm that whips the face and blinds the eyes, there were times when I worried I might not be able to find my way home.

Interrupting our conversation with a kick, our baby girl reminded us of her presence.

"I felt her," I told Jen with a laugh and eyes the size of half-dollars. "I felt Emma kick!" I said again, in a voice of child-like excitement.

And, suddenly, turning from Jen's belly to her eyes, and then back to her belly, my face streamed with tears once again. But this time they were happy tears—only happy tears. I was home.

Afterword

A man travels the world over
in search of what he needs
and returns home to find it.

—Kathleen Norris

When I first left home for Oxford, I went not knowing where the road would lead, but confident this road was the road we were called to take. I was confident of this because, had we not been called, there's no way I would have gone. I was far too comfortable and this journey was far too scary. It was also the opposite of everything I had ever hoped for growing up, and certainly the opposite of Jen's dreams of settling down and starting a family. But it wasn't long before I began to imagine a very specific picture of where this road was leading. And by the time I left Oxford, I was overwhelmed with sadness. Not just from saying good-bye to so many people and places I treasured, but also because the picture I had imagined had not come to fruition. Even after getting to a spot where I was willing to admit my dreams of being a writer, I was leaving Oxford discouraged and without a book deal. I had built castles in the sand, and standing there at the end of this journey, watching the waves wash them away, I wondered what all this meant for my calling.

When I was in Oxford and the doors continued to close on how I thought things were supposed to go, I would often doubt whether I had been called at all. When we were in Paris and I received the email telling me my manuscript didn't have enough of a "hook"; when we were preparing for Thanksgiving dinner at the Kilns and I read the publisher's email telling me they were going to have to pass; when I heard back from publisher after publisher saying, "Thanks, but no thanks"; I felt as though I had failed. I felt as though maybe this whole journey was a failure. *Maybe we were never supposed to have left home in the first place*, I would think to myself in the quiet of the night, staring up at the ceiling in the dark. *Maybe we weren't actually called at all.*

At some point on our journey, I began to believe being called means having clarity about where one is being called. And I began to hold specific expectations for what our journey should look like. But I'm not so sure that's right. Jesus never seems interested in merely satisfying our expectations. The people of Jesus' day expected a powerful political ruler of a Messiah. What they received was a slaughtered lamb. "Jesus always surprises us," I remember Tim Keller saying during his lectures in Oxford. "But he surprises us in *good* ways."

On a walk through Christ Church meadow one sunny spring afternoon in Oxford, my friend Simon the vicar told me in his rich English accent, "I think you'll realize afterward that God brought you here for more than just a degree. He's teaching you both through all of this, and you might not know how until much later."

Simon's words lingered in my ears long after that conversation, and it was only after saying good-bye to England that I began to realize what they might mean. It was only after returning to life in the States that I began to see that our journey to Oxford actually had less to do with Oxford than with what it looks like to follow God's calling. This journey, I would come to realize, had little to do with Oxford, in and of itself, apart from the fact that it just happened to be the place where God taught me what it meant to follow, to say yes.

Much of my journey had been, at its root, the pursuit of an idol. While I had left home, family, and career, certain we were following where God was leading, somewhere along the way I got a very specific idea of what that was supposed to look like. Instead of letting God lead, I began letting my own vision lead. You may pursue an idol by remaining precisely where you are, locked to your safe, comfortable chair by fear of what it might look like to take that first step out in faith. As it turns out, you may also pursue an idol by leaving home and traveling halfway around the world to study theology.

It was only after saying good-bye to Oxford that I began to realize it was possible that this whole journey wasn't as much about C. S. Lewis, Oxford, or even studying theology, as it was about taking this step in faith. And that it was only there, in England, where my grip had been loosed from everything I thought might mean security—my job, my family and friends back home, even the person I loved more than anyone else in the world—that I began to understand what it means to follow

Christ. What it might mean to be called. "God is the great iconoclast," as C. S. Lewis once noted.

———— ❧ ————

"Come, follow me," Jesus says to those who wish to be his disciples, now as then. And if we listen carefully, really carefully, our stomachs turn a somersault and our hearts skip a beat. Because, though he does not stop to tell us where he is leading, we know where he is going. He is going to the cross. And he tells us to drop our nets and follow.

One of the biggest obstacles holding me back before we left home was my fear of going to Oxford and having no promise of security on the other side of this experience. It was a feeling that if I left a great job to go after what I believed God was calling us to, it would be irresponsible. I had a regular paycheck, and life was secure. I had what I had always dreamt of as a kid from a low-income, single-parent family: security. And I shuddered to think I might actually be called to leave that all behind. To me, that felt irresponsible. The truth is, it was only after I took that first step that I realized any provisions we had did not ultimately come from me at all, but only from God. Sometimes we can't see that from where we're standing, but time and time again on this journey, God provided for us in ways I cannot ignore, just as he had before we left.

It was only after this journey that I came to learn that, just as my life is not my own, neither is my calling. I found peace in this realization—or maybe that's where Peace found me.

Nearly a year after leaving Oxford, I found myself in the back row of the social services waiting room in North Carolina. I sat there, beside my wife and our baby girl, with my neck craned back and my head resting against the red brick wall, my eyes moving slowly from face to face around the room. Sitting there, I realized we would not have found ourselves here were it not for feeling called to this journey; had I not let go of all the security I had been chasing, and said, "Okay, I'll go."

"Well, you'll qualify for food stamps, if you're interested," the woman in the worn sweater behind a cluttered desk of papers and family photos said without taking her eyes off her computer screen. Jen's eyes met mine over the top of our daughter's head, her lips turned slightly upward at the corners.

In a strange way, it was only there that I realized, *This is what it means, for me, to be called. This is what it means to follow the living Lord.* Because it was there, with my wife and baby girl sitting next to me, that I properly understood for the first time what this journey had meant. It meant letting go of everything in my life that I thought might give me security, and coming to the realization that such trust ought never be placed in anything but the living Son of God.

Being called by God, I learned, doesn't mean being called to a particular job, school, or even vocation, so much as it means being called to surrender—not just surrendering once, and then returning to our former way of life, but an entire life of surrender. It may involve a deep self-realization along the way—such as when I learned from the community of artists in the San Juan Islands that writing is somehow more central to how God created me than simply something I do—but I am quite certain that calling, Christian calling, is not simply a form of divine wish fulfillment. Christian calling, if it is anything, cannot simply be labeling our own dreams our "calling," and then going after them, come hell or high water. Instead, Christian calling means being called by the living, resurrected Christ to follow him. And it is in following Christ, through continual self-surrender, that we begin to realize who we are, and what it means to walk with God day by day.

But this calling is God's calling on our life, not our own calling. *My* calling is something I possess, which must be fundamentally different than *God's* calling on my life. God's calling on my life is that which I pursue, but never possess nor control. The Christian cannot be self-called.

Day after day, we are called to return to the altar, placing all of our dreams and aspirations there, placing before God's throne even that which we believe to be God's call on our lives. Then we go forth into each day in faith, trust, and hope, to learn what God has for us. Sometimes I wonder if God grants our prayer requests only so that we might, once receiving them, leave them at the altar and follow him. "Never, however, can yesterday decisively influence my moral actions today," wrote the German theologian and pastor Dietrich Bonhoeffer. "I must rather always establish anew my immediate relationship with God's will. I will do something again today not because it seemed the right thing to do yesterday, but because today, too, God's will has pointed me in that direction" ("Basic Question of a Christian Ethic," *Barcelona, Berlin, New York, 1928–1931*, Dietrich Bonhoeffer Works, Vol. 10, 365).

Toward the end of my time in Oxford, I was writing back and forth with an old pastor friend in the States. We were talking about vocation and future plans, about church and my fears regarding security. My friend was telling me he thought the church was in desperate need of people who would love the local body with a Christlike, covenantal love. And then he went on to say something I hope I never forget: "That's probably why Bonhoeffer wrote, 'When God calls a man, he bids him come and die.' That is my prayer for you, Ryan; that you die to Ryan and live for Christ."

To be called, to be a Christian—whether there is any difference, I do not know—is to be called to give up one's life, daily, to the person and vision of God in Christ. I know now, in a way I did not before we left, that such a life is terrifying. It will hurt deeply. But anyone who takes this journey seriously will, no doubt, have to trust God in a way they likely have never done before. And in that trusting, they will come to know God in a way they never have before. For the Christian, every level of security must be subjected to the cross. The posture of the Christian should be a posture of sacrificial suffering. Not self-seeking suffering, but accepting the suffering that inevitably comes when one follows God and loves others in and for Christ. This is what it means to be called. This is what it must mean to be a Christian.

And so we let go of all we hold on to for security, and we follow the living Lord. We drop our nets, those we use for fishing as well as those we have set up to catch us when we fall, and we set out in pursuit of him. We know where he is going, or so we think. He is going to the cross.

Even though I felt as though I had failed by the end of my time in Oxford, I began to realize there was a story here that needed to be told. As Douglas Gresham shared with me on our walk together, it is important to honor the stories God gives us. To retell them, even when it's painful. The truth is, we need each other's stories, to help us as we go. And so I share this story with you not because I think our journey is normative—not everyone is called to leave a job and move halfway around the world. Instead, I do so because I believe we're all called to follow, and because I believe an awful lot of us are deathly afraid to take that first step.

I could not have realized the peaks and valleys our journey would hold before we left; but hopefully by reading our story, you will be more prepared for the story of your own journey. Hopefully you won't be taken off guard when the road you're on suddenly takes an unexpected turn. At times, it will likely include incredible peaks, the kind of experiences you could not have dreamed of before you first stepped out in faith. At other times, your journey will likely entail long, dark valleys that seem to stretch on and on and on.

If you decide to give in to that quiet, itching voice that keeps you up at night, the one that won't relent until you give in and go, know it may very well cost you everything: friends, family, money, and security. And if you decide to give it all up because you believe that's what God is calling you to do, I am no more likely than you are to know where your journey will lead. Maybe it will mean the fulfillment of all your dreams and more. Maybe it will mean closed doors and late-night tears. Maybe, just maybe, it will mean both.

The point of our journey was not Oxford, nor was it writing, in and of itself. I realized that I write not so much because I believed a book deal would somehow make my life complete, but because, even after so many closed doors, I cannot help but write. Because for me, as Parker Palmer describes vocation, writing is that which I can't *not* do. I write because, as Buechner puts it, when I get up in the morning, like it or not, whether it's any good or not, writing is where my feet take me. I write to see the world. I do not quite know what I see, and I certainly don't know what I think, until I've written it. So when I look out at the world, I find myself wanting to trace its contours with words. I write because, when I look out at the world—waking up to winter's first snowfall blanketing our old street in North Oxford, Emma's sideways grin as she learns to smell flowers in Duke Gardens, the last sunset of summer melting behind the San Juan Islands—I want to write it. When I look out at the world, I want to help it; and somehow, I feel as though by writing, I just might.

Being called means not only following the living Lord, but also using the gifts he has given us along the way, in humble obedience. For Doug, who I met on a spring break trip to Maine all those years ago, it meant using his hands and a hammer to build a safe place to call home for women and children whose husbands and fathers used their hands to beat them. For Douglas Gresham, it means continuing to tell stories of his mother and stepfather— two people who mean so much to so many—even if that requires him to relive the crushing feeling of loss. For C. S. Lewis, it meant risking his reputation among colleagues and, even more, his career, as he used his literary talents and sharp mind to teach others that it is okay to believe the story of God's work in our world—believe not just with our hearts, or even our minds, but with our whole lives. For me, it meant leaving behind a job where I wrote marketing campaigns and press releases so that I might string together words like Cheerios on fishing line in my best attempt to help others see him for what he is: the fulfillment of all that we can only begin to glimpse in our best dreams.

I continue to write, even with my forehead bruised and my nose bloodied by the thud of so many closed doors, because it is in my writing that I find myself following God and loving others. I write because it is in my writing that I find myself saying yes, even when I feel like saying no. If I really mean it when I say I am a Christian, if those words mean anything at all, it seems there is no choice but to follow wherever he might lead. This realization does not make me a hero, but it just might make me a Christian. And maybe even called.

Being called means surrendering the story we've been fighting to tell, and to instead accept the story God wants to tell with our lives. His story will be told, no doubt; we do well to submit ourselves to his telling it through us. And there is peace in that. Bonhoeffer calls our submission to God's will "grace" because it means freedom from the chains of a self-chosen way. It is a paradox, but freedom is found in surrender, in giving over our own will to God's leading through the unique gifts and passions he has given each one of us.

"Come, follow me," Jesus says. And so we go—humbly and unsure, dragging our feet, but we go. I pick up my pen and begin again, following wherever he might lead. As my friends Dick and Nigel and the rest of the artists on Orcas Island like to say: *I only have a few pieces of bread and some fish, but here it is. It is yours.* He intends to make with it a feast.

———————— ❧ ————————

Surrendering often looks like throwing in the towel. It looks like failure. But it is not. In the end, it is the only path for us, you and me. To be sure, the cross looks like failure to the world, and yet, to us, to those who would hear the call and follow, it is life.

When the living Lord calls us by name, we are overcome with fear because we know where he's going, and we know that where he's going means death. But we also know something else. We know stories about Easter Sunday and that where Jesus is going also, surprisingly, means life—new life. The kind of life we could not have imagined before we took that first step. The kind of life we could not have manufactured if we tried. The kind of life that's at once exciting and scary. Following Jesus feels like losing control, and then coming to the realization that control was never ours in the first place. I once heard the theologian Stanley Hauerwas tell a room full of divinity school students waiting to graduate: "To love the Lord means to give up control. To lose oneself. To feel out of control. To remind you, you are not your own."

The kind of life God wants to give us can be found only in following him, precisely because it is his life.

From a young age, I believed that if I worked really hard, I could achieve the kind of security I had always dreamed of. And, even more, I believed this security would make me whole. I didn't have a father at home who my friends could know, whose work or name I could point to for my own benefit. I had to go it on my own. And so I did. In other words, I believed the lie of self-sufficiency, which I continued to believe long after my Christian conversion. I worked as hard as I could, with the rewards of good grades, favoritism from teachers, and scholarships all fueling my belief that I could do it on my own. After college, coworkers called me the "golden child," and men years ahead of me assured me I had big things in store. Success followed success, all the way to Oxford. But there, my dreams of success began to unravel.

Particularly in North America, we love stories of people pulling themselves up out of nothing, by their own bootstraps. For me, it wasn't until I arrived in Oxford that my bootstraps snapped, and with them went my belief that an attitude of self-sufficiency could coexist with Christianity. It could not, I would learn. And it was only when I had learned that lesson that I began to experience the peace Christ offers, perhaps for the first time in my life.

In a strange way that I will probably never be able to properly explain, a peace surrounded me on that afternoon in the social services offices, the place that represented everything I had spent my entire short life running from. It was the kind of peace that's only properly described as surpassing all understanding. The kind of peace that puts a smile on your face when you might otherwise feel like crying. The kind of peace that makes you kiss your wife on her forehead, the wife who knows just as well as you do the price this journey has cost, and whose eyes and feigned smile knew something of what this would mean when we first received the letter from Oxford all those years ago. It's the kind of peace that makes you smile at your daughter, with her apple-cheeked grin staring back up at you, knowing, for the first time, this is what it means to follow the living Christ. This is what it means to be called. And this feeling of unspeakable peace is, in some way, a glimmer of what it means to have the new life God offers. It means, in a way that simply doesn't make any sense, that I wouldn't have it any other way.

From the outside looking in, this scene looks like failure. And that's exactly what I would have concluded had someone told me before we set out on this journey that this is where our travels would take us. But the cross has always looked like failure from the outside. And yet, for those who receive his voice with ears that hear, for those who recognize themselves as called, for those who follow, Jesus bids us come and die. Seated there thinking about all we had given up, I couldn't help but feel like, in some strange way, this was precisely where we were supposed to be. I couldn't help but feel as though our journey had just begun.

We've begun packing. Pictures are being taken off the walls; boxes labeled with black felt-tipped markers are being filled with dishes and baby blankets and toys. I'll be sending this manuscript to my editor soon. And then, we'll stuff the last of our things in a U-Haul—all our possessions from Washington, as well as a few things we've picked up along the way in England, Rome, Paris, and North Carolina—and we'll make the cross-country drive. I'm hoping to stare down into the belly of the Grand Canyon; I've never seen it before. In a couple months, friends and family will gather around cake as we celebrate Emma's second birthday. She has the same smile that stole my heart in our high school auditorium all those years ago. Her chocolate-brown curls are now nearly touching her shoulders.

Very soon, we'll be moving back to the same small town where I grew up, with the same snow-capped mountains, and the same baseball fields where I once stood with a mitt on my hand, just wishing my dad were there to watch. I do not now know what the next chapter holds for us. I do not know what I will be doing after we get there.

If I were being honest, I'd tell you I could not be more scared. But I'd also tell you I could not be more excited. In a strange way, in a way I would never have believed before we set out on this journey, I cannot help but feel this is precisely where we're being called.

———————————— ❧ ————————————

Frederick Buechner once wrote, "My story is important not because it is mine, God knows, but because if I tell it anything like right, the chances are you will recognize that in many ways it is also yours. . . . [I]t is precisely through these stories in all their particularity, as I have long believed and often said, that God makes himself known to each of us more powerfully and personally" (*Telling Secrets* 9).

I hope I am never so naïve as to think the journey of a twentysomething and his wife who left home, community, and their jobs is somehow prescriptive for all Christians everywhere. And yet my hope is that, in some way I could never guess, you might see your own story in our story, and know what it means for you to be called, to go, and to follow where he is leading.

Maybe for you being called means following God by staying where you are, but in a way you never have before; by using the gifts and passions God has given you in a way you may never have imagined; in a way that looks crazy to those on the outside, but which you know is exactly where God would have you. It will look crazy to others because it will mean, quite possibly for the first time, handing over your whole heart. Or maybe, just maybe, your story will resemble ours. Maybe for you, following God will involve leaving everything and going, not knowing exactly where the road is leading, but knowing the road you're on is the road where he is leading you. Whatever it may look like, the important thing is that you follow—that you loosen your grip on all of the gifts and passions he has given you, everything that makes up you, and that you hand it over to him and to the story he is telling. And that when he calls, you go, even if going means staying. Beautiful things happen when God's people "go."

If you go, you will likely wake up one day more glad than you've ever been that you took that first step, but also more scared than you've ever been for doing so. On that day, take comfort. Know you are precisely where God would have you. You are on a journey of unspeakable peaks and incredible valleys, but a journey that will, no doubt, lead you to him.

"For whoever would save his life will lose it," Jesus told the crowds of his day, just as he tells us. "But whoever loses his life for *my* sake will find it" (Matt. 16:25, emphasis added).

Acknowledgments

A very special thank you to Amanda, my literary agent, for taking me on all those years ago. Thanks for sticking with me through all the closed doors. Even more, thank you for reminding me that you don't just believe in my writing, but in me. You are a gem.

Thank you to the folks at Leafwood for saying yes to this book. Thank you, Gary, for your excitement, and for all your help bringing it to birth. Thank you, Mary, for your precise eye and your tireless attention. And many thanks to all those at Leafwood who have helped prepare this book for its big day. Thanks also to ThinkPen Design for the stunning cover; what a gift.

Thanks to those at Oxford and Duke whose work and thought undeniably found its way into these pages: Philip Kennedy, Matthew Kirkpatrick, Michael Ward, Stanley Hauerwas, Rick Lischer, Willie Jennings, J. Kameron Carter, C. Kavin Rowe. Luke Powery, thanks for so many lunches and conversations.

Called

Thank you to the C. S. Lewis Foundation for allowing me to live at the Kilns, where much of this writing took place, and where so many dreams came true.

Thanks to Liz for allowing me to use her Writing as Spiritual Formation course at Duke Divinity to carve away time for this manuscript in the midst of finishing my degree. Thanks also to Doug and Carol for the best writing space anyone could ask for. Thanks to Sigur Rós, Jónsi, The National, Daughter, Ryan Adams, Bon Iver, Mat Kearney, the Brilliance, and Augustines for the soundtrack to these words.

Thank you to all the writers whose work helped show me the way: Frederick Buechner, Donald Miller, Lauren Winner, Anne Lamott, Annie Dillard, and, of course, C. S. Lewis. As J. I. Packer once put it, "Thank you, Mr. Lewis, for being you. I wouldn't have missed you for the world."

Thank you to Tim and Kathy Keller. Thank you to Douglas Gresham. You shared your life with me in a way that helped bring this book into being.

This story is told through the lens of my life, which obviously involves many other lives. Thank you to all those who allowed me to tell the painful and exciting stories of our overlapping journeys. Zach and Goose. Ben and Leann. Thank you, Mom. Thank you, Dad. I love you both, and I so appreciate your love and support along the way. Tim and Rhonda, thank you for all you've done to support this journey. Even more, thank you for trusting me with the story of Hayley's loss, fragile as it is. The grace with which you have handled this pain is beyond admirable.

Thanks to all the friends who encouraged my writing, long before *Called* was even an idea: Jen, Pastor Craig, Brian and Jen, Doug and Lora, Tawni, David, John, Chris, J. D., and Craig.

Thank you, Doug and Carol; how indebted I am to you for your friendship, for your wisdom, for your love. Thank you to my dear friend and first publisher, Steve. It is hard to imagine much of this happening without you. Thank you to Jon and Allison for introducing me to Lewis's writing all those years ago. Thank you to those who unknowingly reminded me of the story I was trying to tell when I became a stranger to myself: Lucy, Aaron, Grandpa, and Hayley. And thanks to all the friends made along the journey who brought light into my life, and in so helping me, helped these words: Cole, Walter, Bryan and Freya, Olli and Salla, Rich, Max, Britton, Jason, Tom, Jarred and Chelsea, Spud, Jonathan, Dom, Lyndon and Mim, Rob and Vanessa, Penn and Grace, Tyler and Lauren, Laura, Professor Steve, Kaili, Dick and Nigel, Kendall, Russ and Malissa, Jay and Anne, and, with very special thanks, Todd and Emily. Thanks to Debbie for leftover soup and warm cookies. Thank you, Gary, for your words of experience along the way. Thank you to my friends at Duke who were invaluable proofreaders: Elliott, Katie, and Sarah. Thanks also to Laura, Brett, Jason, and John for reading early drafts. It is embarrassing how much better this book is because of your help. Thank you to all those who prayed over this journey, and who pray still.

Thank you, wherever you might be, for taking the time to read these words. You are not likely to know just how much it means. I look forward to thanking you in person one day.

Penultimately, thank you to two girls who I cannot imagine life without. Emma, your life has brought me life when I needed it most. And Jen, you were tough when I wasn't. You had faith when I didn't. You urged me to keep going when, by all accounts, it should have been the other way around. Quite simply, without you, these words would not be. Here, in your hands, is my heart. It is yours.

Lastly, thank you to the One who calls out still, "Follow Me;" in whose name alone there is peace and life; and whose in-breaking light means our hope. To him be the glory, now and forever. Amen.